Apples of Gold in Silver Settings

Apples of Gold in Silver Settings

... And 30 Other Bible-Based Meditations

Series # 10

Roger Ellsworth

Unless otherwise noted, Scripture quotations are taken from the New King James Version®. Copyright © 1982 by Thomas Nelson. Used by permission. All rights reserved.

Copyright © 2018, Roger Ellsworth

All rights reserved. No part of this book may be reproduced, scanned, or distributed in any printed or electronic form without permission.

First Edition: 2018

ISBN: 978-0-9600203-0-0

20181115LS

Great Writing Publications
www.greatwriting.org
Taylors, SC

www.greatwriting.org

Purpose

My Coffee Cup Meditations are short, easy-to-read, engagingly presented devotions based on the Bible, the Word of God. Each reading takes a single idea or theme and develops it in a thought-provoking way so that you are inspired to consider the greatness of God, the relevance of the good news of the life, death, resurrection, and coming-again of Jesus, and are better equipped for life in this world and well prepared for the world to come.

www.mycoffeecupmeditations.com

https://www.facebook.com/MyCoffeeCupMeditations/

Dedication

To

Bobby and Jeanette Holt

About This Book

This book is the result of the labors Roger Ellsworth and the thought he has given to various passages of Scripture over the years. You may read more about Roger on page 141.

We hope you will enjoy these Bible-based meditations. We would love to hear from you, so please send us a note to tell us what you think—which ones you liked most, and how they made a difference in your life or in the life of a family member, friend, or work associate. To reach us online, go to
www.mycoffeecupmeditations.com/contact

MY COFFEE-CUP MEDITATIONS

Table of Contents

1 Apples of Gold in Silver Settings 16
2 God Speaks to Satan 20
3 The Son Speaks to the Father 24
4 An Angel Speaks to Joseph 28
5 The Father Speaks from Heaven 32
6 The First Words of Jesus' Ministry 36
7 "I Am the Bread of Life" (Jesus) 40
8 "I Am the Light of the World" (Jesus) 44
9 "I Am the Door" (Jesus) 48
10 "I Am the Good Shepherd" (Jesus) 52
11 "I Am the Resurrection and the Life" (Jesus) 56
12 "I Am the Way, the Truth and the Life" (Jesus) 60
13 "I Am the Vine" (Jesus) 64
14 Jesus Speaks to His Father 68
15 "Father, Forgive Them. . ." (Jesus) 72
16 "Today, You Will Be with Me in Paradise" (Jesus) 76
17 "Woman, Behold Your Son" (Jesus) 80
18 "My God, My God, Why Have You Forsaken Me?" (Jesus).. 84
19 "I Thirst" (Jesus) 88
20 "It is Finished!" (Jesus) 92
21 "Father, into Your Hands I Commit My Spirit" (Jesus) 96
22 A Centurion Speaks about Jesus 100
23 "He is Not Here" (Two Angels) 104
24 "This Same Jesus. . . Will So Come" (An Angel) 108
25 Paul Speaks to a Jailer 112

26 The Next-to-Last Words of Jesus	116
27 A Word from the Holy Spirit	120
28 The Last Words of Jesus	124
29 An Apple of Gold from a Rotten Apple (1)	128
30 An Apple of Gold from a Rotten Apple (2)	132
31 A Truly Rotten Apple from a Truly Rotten Apple	136
About the Author	141
The Series	142

The App

www.mycoffeecupmeditations.com

Be sure you get the app!

-1-

From God's Word, the Bible...

A word fitly spoken is like apples of gold
In settings of silver.

Proverbs 25:11

Apples of Gold in Silver Settings

A word "fitly spoken" is the appropriate word. It's the right word for the occasion. It's the word that fits. It's the word that causes us to say: "Yes, that's it. There's nothing else to say."

The Bible reports many fitly spoken words. All of the Bible's words are true and significant, but I'm talking about those instances in which the Bible actually reports what someone had to say to another person or to other people.

In the readings that follow, we will notice some words that God the Father spoke. Fit words they were! We will also notice many of the words that the Lord Jesus spoke. Wonderful words indeed! There will be a reading on a word that the Holy Spirit actually spoke as well as some readings on words that angels spoke. And, of course, we will want to notice some fitly words spoken by human beings.

I trust that each of these readings will seem to you to be as an apple of gold in a setting of silver.

I've seen gold, and I've seen silver, but I have never seen apples of gold in silver settings. My initial reaction is that such apples in such settings must reflect both tremendous value and exquisite beauty.

There are words like that. Words of tremendous value and exquisite beauty! And we can possess them even though they were all spoken so very long ago. We can possess them by reading the reports of them in the Bible and by reflecting deeply on what we have read. If we don't read these things and reflect on them, we are depriving ourselves of both their value and their beauty.

For words to be like apples of gold in silver settings, they have to deal with matters of great importance. One can speak a fit word even when trivial matters are being discussed, but that surely wouldn't qualify as an apple of gold in a setting of silver.

The words that will receive our attention in the readings that follow are truly valuable because they all have some connection with the one matter of supreme importance, namely, God's plan of salvation. We might say they all have some connection with the matter of receiving eternal life. No other words can compare to these. Simon Peter, who so often said the wrong thing, said exactly the right thing when he spoke these words to Jesus: "Lord, to whom shall we go? You have the words of eternal life" (John 6:68).

That was certainly a word fitly spoken. It was an apple of gold in a silver setting.

In the early 1870s, Fleming H. Revell (Dwight Moody's brother-in-law) was in the process of launching a Christian publication that was to be called *Words of Life*. Mr. Revell persuaded Philip Bliss to write a hymn that would be appropriate for the first issue. In 1874, that issue was released with this hymn from Bliss:

> *Sing them over again to me,*
> *Wonderful words of life;*
> *Let me more of their beauty see,*
> *Wonderful words of life;*
> *Words of life and beauty,*
> *Teach me faith and duty:*
> *Beautiful words, wonderful words,*
> *Wonderful words of life;*
> *Beautiful words, wonderful words,*
> *Wonderful words of life.*

A few short months after writing that hymn, Philip Bliss and his wife entered into the life of which he had so often written, dying in a train wreck in Ohio in December of 1876.

Because Philip Bliss' hymn celebrated the wonderful words that lead us to eternal life, I would call it an apple of gold in a setting of silver.

Bliss was only thirty-eight when he died. This life is so very unpredictable. It can end very quickly and plunge us out into eternity. How very many there are who are speeding toward it without giving any thought to it!

In *The Pilgrim's Progress*, John Bunyan has the pilgrim leaving the City of Destruction, crying as he runs down the path: "Eternal life! Eternal life!" We would do well to do as the pilgrim did. We would do well to prize eternal life above all else. We would do well to read and heed the words that God, angels, and men have spoken about eternal life. Like apples of gold in settings of silver, they are words of enormous value and beauty.

-2-

From God's Word, the Bible...

*"And I will put enmity
Between you and the woman,
And between your seed and her Seed;
He shall bruise your head,
And you shall bruise His heel."*

Genesis 3:15

God Speaks to Satan

Everything now seemed so bleak! So grim! Adam and Eve thought that disobeying God would bring them happiness. It didn't. They didn't realize what they had done. Through their disobedience they had essentially broken their friendship with God and formed a new friendship with Satan—a ghastly friendship!

God could have left it that way. He could have let this new friendship stand. But God came after His disobedient creatures, found them, and announced that He was going to break their new friendship. He would destroy their friendship with the devil and restore them to friendship with Himself.

It's all recorded right there in Genesis 3:15. God says to Satan (who had appeared as a serpent):

> *I will put enmity*
> *Between you and the woman. . . .*

Enmity is the opposite of friendship. Satan had used the

woman to destroy friendship with God (vv. 1-6); God would use her to restore that friendship.

How would God use the woman to restore friendship with Himself? Through her would come the "Seed." Notice the singular. God would restore sinners to friendship with Himself through one person being born of a woman. The fact that God was referring to one person is established when the Lord goes on to say: "He shall. . ."

Who is this person who would be born of a woman for the purpose of undoing what the devil had done? It is none other than the Lord Jesus Christ (Gal. 4:4). Amazing thing! He, the Second Person of the Trinity, would actually be born of a woman! He would take our humanity!

What we have here is God saying to Satan: "You used the man I put here to destroy My friendship. I'm going to send another Man, another Adam, to undo what you have done. You have succeeded with My first Adam. Let's see how you do with the Second Adam."

How Satan hated this announcement! How he hated Jesus, the Seed of the woman! And how he stirred up hostility against Him!

Coming to this earth in our humanity was certainly an amazing thing, but it wasn't enough to actually restore sinners to friendship with God. To do that, Jesus had to die on the cross, and, yes, the cross is found here in Genesis 3:15. It's in these words:

> *He shall bruise your head,*
> *And you shall bruise His heel.*

The hatred of Satan for Jesus would culminate in Jesus being crucified. That cross looked to be a stunning victory for Satan. Jesus had come, and Satan had won! That's how it appeared. But Satan's "victory" was only the bruising of

Jesus' heel. That cross which appeared to be Satan's victory was in fact Jesus' victory. It consisted of Jesus bringing His bruised heel down with crushing force on Satan's head!

How did Jesus' death on the cross defeat Satan? What happened there to break the friendship of sinners with Satan and to restore them to friendship with God? It paid the penalty of sin. Sin is the chain that binds sinners to Satan. What a friendship—one that uses a chain!

Jesus died on the cross to pay the penalty for sinners. His death broke the chain. With sin's penalty paid, Satan no longer had the chain with which to bind sinners to himself in "friendship."

Adam and Eve were restored to life's true friendship, friendship with God, by looking forward in faith to the coming and dying of the Lord Jesus Christ.

Adam's sin caused all of his descendants to be born as sinners. All of us come into this world in a state of friendship with Satan and alienation toward God. But it doesn't have to stay that way. We can enter into friendship with God by looking in faith to the redeeming work of the Lord Jesus. Adam and Eve looked forward to Christ, we look backward to Christ, but being saved has always been, is and always will be, a matter of looking to Christ.

If I were asked to make a list of the most amazing words ever spoken, I would have to begin with the words God spoke in Genesis 3:15. I would like to have been there to have heard those words. They announced the way for me to be forgiven of my sins and restored to friendship with God. What wonderful words! But I didn't have to hear them when they were spoken because I can hear them now as I read this verse. For that, I'm thankful.

-3-

From God's Word, the Bible...

Sacrifice and offering You did not desire;
My ears You have opened.
Burnt offering and sin offering You did not require.
Then I said, "Behold, I come;
In the scroll of the book it is written of me.
I delight to do Your will, O my God,
And Your law is within my heart."

Psalm 40:6-8

The Son Speaks to the Father

Have you ever wished you could have listened in on a highly significant conversation? Have you ever wished you could have been a fly on the wall in the innermost chambers of highly influential people as they discussed crucial matters? These verses make us that fly on the wall. They enable us to hear one side of the greatest of all conversations.

David, the king of Israel, reports this half of the conversation to us. But while he wrote these words, they aren't really his words. The Spirit of God carried David to such a high level that he was enabled to write the words of the Lord Jesus Himself. David was here serving as the mouthpiece of the Messiah.

To whom did the Messiah speak these words? There can be no doubt about that. They are addressed to God the Father. Note the phrase "O my God" in verse 8.

The Father had given His Son a task. This was no small

task! It was to accomplish that work which all the sacrifices of the Old Testament era could never accomplish. Those sacrifices, while ordained by God, could only paint a picture of salvation for sinners. They could never actually provide it. The work of salvation was still awaiting the doing. And now we have the Lord Jesus declaring that He was coming to do the work. He says to the Father: "Behold, I come."

When did Jesus speak these words? The answer that leaps to mind is when He was ready to leave the courts of heaven to enter this realm in our humanity.

It should be plain to us that the three persons of the Trinity were united on this matter of redeeming sinners. It was the Holy Spirit who prompted David to write about redemption. It was the Father's will to save sinners by sending His Son. And the Son didn't reluctantly, grudgingly take up the work. Not for a moment! He says:

> *I delight to do Your will, O my God,*
> *And Your law is within my heart.*
> (v. 8)

What does it mean to be a sinner? It means we are law breakers. We refuse to keep God's laws and insist on going our own way. Our law breaking disqualifies us from entering heaven because God demands that we be perfectly righteous to enter there. Thank God for Jesus. The law we so deeply despise and so frequently break, He embraced with all of His heart. And He perfectly kept it. In doing so, He provided for us that perfect righteousness which God demands.

After living that life of perfect obedience, Jesus went to the cross to receive the penalty of our law breaking. Here is the gospel in a nutshell—Jesus got our sins so that all who believe in Him may have His righteousness.

What is this "scroll of the Book" which Jesus mentions? Some think it refers to the Old Testament, all of which points forward to the coming of Christ and the work of salvation that He would achieve. Others think this scroll takes us all the way back to that time even before the world began when the Father, the Son, and the Holy Spirit entered into agreement with each other about the work of redemption and wrote it all down.

It's really not necessary for us to choose between these two possibilities because each is true. It is true that the three persons of the Trinity agreed with each other on the details of redemption before the world began. And it is true that the Old Testament prophesied the work of Christ. Let's refuse to choose, and let's rejoice in both!

What a conversation we have depicted in these verses! The Father must have said: "Son, here is the work of redemption that You must do!" And the Son responded: "Yes, Father, I will take up the work. I will gladly and fully do it to the last detail."

Jesus' side of this conversation expressed His commitment to our salvation. Because of His commitment—one He didn't have to make—all who repent of their sins and trust in Him have forgiveness for their sins and eternal life.

-4-

From God's Word, the Bible...

But while he thought about these things, behold, an angel of the Lord appeared to him in a dream, saying, "Joseph, son of David, do not be afraid to take to you Mary your wife, for that which is conceived in her is of the Holy Spirit. And she will bring forth a Son, and you shall call His name Jesus, for He will save His people from their sins."

Matthew 1:20-21

An Angel Speaks to Joseph

Mary was pregnant, and her fiancé Joseph was perplexed. The child wasn't his. Assuming Mary had been unfaithful to him, he was inclined to break their engagement quietly, that is, without subjecting Mary to the legal procedures of that time.

Then everything changed for Joseph in an instant. An angel suddenly appeared to him in a dream to offer an explanation and to give an instruction.

The explanation had to do with Mary's pregnancy. It was unique. There had not been one like this before. The angel said: ". . . that which is conceived in her is of the Holy Spirit" (v. 20).

The instruction had to do with the naming of the One who was to be born. The angel said to Joseph: ". . . you shall call His name JESUS, for He will save His people from their sins" (v. 21).

I love the name "Jesus" because it means "salvation,"

and this I know about myself: I need salvation. What is it that I need to be saved from? The angel made it clear. I need to be saved from my sins. And what I have said about myself is true of everyone. We are all sinners (Rom. 3:23), and we all need to be saved from our sins.

Jesus came to this earth for the express purpose of providing salvation for sinners, and there would be no such salvation had He not come.

Yes, Jesus provides an example for us on the matter of how we should live, but that wasn't the primary reason that He came. Jesus was certainly a marvelous teacher, but He didn't come to only be a teacher. Jesus came to be the Savior. Any explanation for Him other than that comes woefully short of the truth about the Lord Jesus.

To say that Jesus came to this earth to save sinners is to say that He came to pay the penalty that those sinners deserve. God's holy character precludes Him from forgiving sinners without that penalty being paid. God would sin against Himself if He were to ignore the penalty that He Himself had pronounced on sin. So the huge question was this: how could God at one and the same time carry out the penalty that He had pronounced on sinners and let those very same sinners go free? To put it another way, how could God both punish and not punish sinners? Or, to put it yet another way, how could God simultaneously satisfy His justice that demanded payment for sin and His grace that demanded release for sinners? Enormous dilemma!

Now you know why I love the name "Jesus." He is the answer to God's dilemma. On the cross, He received the penalty that God's justice required. What a penalty it was! It was the penalty of eternal separation from God, and Jesus experienced that on the cross. That's why He cried: "My God, My God, why have You forsaken Me?" (Matt. 27:46).

Because He was God, an infinite person, He could

receive an eternity's worth of wrath in a finite measure of time. Amazing!

Justice looked on the cross of Jesus and clapped its hands in approval because the demand that it made against sinners was fully carried out. But grace looked on that same cross and clapped its hands as well for this reason: because Jesus had paid the penalty, there was no penalty left for those sinners who trust in Him. Justice and grace met in Jesus.

Now you see the reason I love the name "Jesus." But I have to say there's another word that I love in the angel's announcement. It is the word "will." That's a definite word. It doesn't allow for uncertainty. Jesus was coming to this earth to provide salvation for sinners, and He would succeed in that work. Nothing would stop Him.

I would have enjoyed hearing the angel speak his words of explanation and instruction to Joseph because those words pertain to something that pertains to me—salvation from my sins. There is nothing greater to be found, and it's all found in Jesus.

We have heard the joyful sound:
Jesus saves! Jesus saves!
Spread the tidings all around:
Jesus saves! Jesus saves!

-5-

From God's Word, the Bible...

And suddenly a voice came from heaven, saying, "This is My beloved Son, in whom I am well pleased."

While he was still speaking, behold, a bright cloud overshadowed them; and suddenly a voice came out of the cloud, saying, "This is My beloved Son, in whom I am well pleased. Hear Him!"

"Father, glorify Your name."
Then a voice came from heaven, saying, "I have both glorified it and will glorify it again."

Matthew 3:17; 17:5; John 12:28

The Father Speaks from Heaven

Three times! That's how often the Father spoke audibly from heaven during His Son's earthly ministry as recorded in the Gospels.

The first of these instances occurred immediately after Jesus was baptized by John the Baptist in the Jordan River.

John's baptism was intended to be an outward expression or picture of genuine repentance for sin (Matt. 3:6,8,11). Jesus showed up one day and asked John to baptize Him. So we're faced with a mystery. If John's baptism was intended to signal repentance of sin, why would Jesus, who never sinned, need to be baptized?

John the Baptist was certainly shocked by Jesus' request. He knew the truth about Jesus. He knew that He was the spotless Lamb of God who had no sin. If there was no sin in Jesus, there was no need for repentance, and, therefore, no need for baptism.

But while Jesus Himself had no sin, He came to save

sinners. In order to save sinners, He had to be their substitute. He had to be the sin-bearer. By standing with John in the waters of the Jordan, Jesus was identifying with the sinners He came to save. He was presenting Himself as their substitute. He was standing with them in their sinfulness, even though He had no sins.

It's interesting that each Person of the Trinity was there at the Jordan River. Jesus, the Son, was there to be baptized. The Spirit of God was there to descend upon Him (Matt. 3:16), and the Father was there to express His approval of His Son (Matt. 3:17). The Father had sent His Son to take the place of sinners as their sin-bearer. So the Father was pleased to see the baptism of His Son.

The second time the Father spoke from heaven was also in approval of His Son. On a mountaintop with three of His disciples, Jesus was suddenly "transfigured before them" (Matt. 17:2) and stood there with Moses and Elijah (Matt. 17:3). We might say Jesus temporarily pulled back the robe of His humanity so the glory of His deity could be clearly seen.

Jesus, Moses, and Elijah didn't simply appear together. They also talked. And what did they talk about? Luke tells us that they "spoke of His decease which He was about to accomplish at Jerusalem" (Luke 9:31).

The fact that Moses, the representative of the Law, and Elijah, the representative of the prophets, spoke to Jesus about His upcoming death shows us that His death fulfilled both the Law and the prophets. His death wasn't merely something that would *happen* to Him. It was something that He would "accomplish." It was the work that He had come to do, and He would do it.

The baptism of Jesus had to do with the cross, and the Transfiguration had to do with the cross. And each time, God the Father spoke from heaven to express His approval.

The Father and the Son were in agreement on the work of the cross. The Father sent the Son to die for sinners, and Jesus came to do as the Father willed.

The third time that the Father spoke from heaven during Jesus' earthly ministry is reported in John's Gospel. On this occasion, the Father spoke in response to Jesus' prayer: "Father, glorify Your name" (John 12:28).

The Father spoke to say that He had both glorified His name and would glorify it again.

We should note that this instance of the Father speaking was also connected with Jesus' death on the cross (John 12:23-24). We might expect Jesus to say: "The hour has come that the Son of Man should be crucified." Instead He said the hour had come for Him to be "glorified."

That shameful, ignominious cross would bring glory to both the Son and the Father. The glory of what Jesus was going to do there would be far greater than the shame He would suffer there. That cross would display the justice, the grace, and the wisdom of God, and, in doing so, would glorify God. That cross would save sinners, and, in doing so, would bring glory to God. The glory of the cross is greater than the sin that made it necessary.

It would certainly have been an awesome thing to hear the Father speak from heaven on those three occasions. But it is an even greater thing to embrace by faith the cross of Christ that received the approval of the Father.

-6-

From God's Word, the Bible...

Now after John was put in prison, Jesus came to Galilee, preaching the gospel of the kingdom of God, and saying, "The time is fulfilled, and the kingdom of God is at hand. Repent, and believe in the gospel."

Mark 1:14-15

The First Words of Jesus' Ministry

After He was tempted in the wilderness, the Lord Jesus went into Galilee where He began "preaching the kingdom of God."

With that message, the Lord struck the keynote for His entire ministry. The four Gospels include over a hundred references to this matter of the kingdom of God. This was the very centerpiece of Jesus' teaching and preaching, and of all that He did.

As we read the opening words of Jesus' ministry, we should be impressed with *the definiteness of them*. Jesus came preaching (v. 14). The word "preaching" takes us to the days in which a king would make important announcements through his herald. The herald would blow a trumpet to get the attention of the people and then announce the news.

This type of thing was always definite. Martyn Lloyd-Jones observes:

> A herald does not make an uncertain announcement, or get up and blow his trumpet and say, "Listen, we do not quite know what's happening nor what is going to take place, but, well, we only hope that something is going to happen!" That is not heralding! [1]

Our time is very hostile to definiteness in religion. We welcome it in other areas. We want our physicians to be definite and precise in their treatment of us. We want our mechanics to be definite and precise in repairing our cars. But we don't like definiteness in religion because with it come clear responsibilities and painful guilt when we fail in those responsibilities. We want everyone, no matter what he believes and how he behaves, to be right on this matter of religion.

The Lord Jesus came with a very definite message about the kingdom of God. He didn't come saying: "All opinions are equally valid on this matter of God's kingdom. Everyone is right, and no one is wrong."

The very fact that Jesus came preaching indicates that His message about the kingdom was very definite and precise.

We should also take note of *the element of good news in Jesus' announcement*.

What Jesus had to say about the kingdom of God was indescribably wonderful. What made it so? The kingdom of God refers to His sovereign rule over His people. It is that rule that frees them from the rule of sin, achieves their complete salvation, makes them part of the community of faith, and conveys them to eternal glory.

We can't appreciate how good this news is until we realize that we don't come into this world as part of God's kingdom, but rather as part of Satan's kingdom, which is the

---

[1] D. Martyn Lloyd-Jones, *The Kingdom of God*, Crossway Books, 1992, p. 12.

kingdom of sin, darkness, and eternal ruin.

To get into God's kingdom, we must be taken out of Satan's. The good news is this: through Christ, God takes sinners out of Satan's kingdom and makes them citizens of His own.

A third element in Jesus' proclamation of God's kingdom is *His indispensable role in it*.

Jesus came saying that His presence meant God's kingdom was "at hand." That didn't mean that it didn't exist before this. God was delivering people from their sins and sovereignly ruling over them before Jesus came. If that hadn't been true, the people who lived before Jesus came were hopelessly lost. God's kingdom was operating in the Old Testament era but in a borrowed sense, that is, borrowed against the future. People were saved by looking forward in faith to what God would eventually do in His Son to deal with their sin. In Mark 1:15, Jesus was declaring that there was no more need to look forward to the coming of the Savior—He was the Savior! He had come to break Satan's rule over sinners and to bring them under the rule of God.

As we look back, we see that the way Jesus did this was by dying on the cross as the substitute for sinners, receiving God's wrath in their stead so they wouldn't have to receive it.

The final element in Jesus' proclamation of the kingdom is *the proper response to it*—"Repent and believe in the gospel." To repent means to turn around. It means we turn from our sins to God. To believe the gospel is to rest our hope for eternal salvation on what the Lord Jesus came to do.

Jesus certainly began His ministry with fitly spoken words. As we read them, we see them to be an "apple of gold."

-7-

From God's Word, the Bible...

And Jesus said to them, "I am the bread of life. He who comes to Me shall never hunger, and he who believes in Me shall never thirst."

"I am the bread of life."

John 6:35, 48

"I Am the Bread of Life" (Jesus)

The Bible tells us that no one ever spoke like Jesus (John 7:46). How very blessed we are to be able to read in the Gospel accounts some of the many words He spoke! While we treasure those accounts, it's okay for us to wonder what it would have been like to hear those words as they fell from Jesus' lips.

Those who are familiar with John's Gospel know that it contains seven "I am" sayings from Jesus. I sometimes wish I could hurl myself through time and hear Him make each of those claims.

The first of them Jesus stated twice: "I am the bread of life." He spoke those words to people who were obsessively concerned with physical bread. On the previous day, He miraculously multiplied bread to satisfy their hunger (vv. 1-14).

Some of that multitude followed Him to Capernaum. Always able to read men, Jesus knew the reason for their interest in Him. They wanted more bread. They were being driven by their desire for "the food which perishes" (v. 27). They were primarily interested in food that would sustain physical life. Meanwhile, they were oblivious to their far greater need, which was food that could produce and sustain spiritual and eternal life.

Jesus' message to them was plain. There is a food, which, if eaten, will produce "everlasting life" (v. 27).

Life that never ends! That's something that I can certainly use! This life passes so swiftly! The years come and go with blinding speed, and then death comes to carry us away. Henry F. Lyte got it right: "Swift to its close ebbs out life's little day."

So I'm very interested in eating that food that will give me life that will never end. What is that food? It is the Lord Jesus Christ. He is the bread of life. He came to this earth from heaven for this very reason—to give "life to the world" (v. 33).

How do we know Jesus came from heaven? All we have to do is look at the many miracles that He performed. They tell us the truth about Him.

The people to whom He was speaking in John 6 had seen Jesus miraculously multiply physical food. That alone gave them sufficient reason to believe that Jesus was from heaven and could give them eternal life. Sadly enough, they all walked away from Him (v. 66). They spurned His offer of eternal life even though they had indisputable evidence that Jesus could give it to them. Their interest in physical life crowded out interest in eternal life.

What did Jesus do to provide eternal life? To put it another way, what makes Jesus the bread that produces eternal life? He gives us the answer in these words: ". . . the bread that I shall give is My flesh, which I shall give for the life of the world" (v. 51).

Jesus was talking about His death on the cross. That is where He gave His flesh and shed His blood, and that death is the thing that makes Him the bread of life, that makes it possible for Him to give us spiritual and eternal life. By dying on the cross, Jesus dealt with the thing that keeps us from having spiritual and eternal life—sin. On the cross, He received the penalty for sin, and, in doing so, took sin out of the way so it can no longer keep us from having spiritual and eternal life.

Jesus is the bread of life by virtue of His death on the cross. But Jesus, the bread, has to be eaten. How do we "eat" Jesus? In some verses, the Lord Jesus tells us that we must eat His flesh and drink His blood if we are to have eternal life (vv. 53-58). In other verses, He tells us that we must believe in Him if we are to have eternal life (vv. 29, 35, 40, 47). The point is quite clear. To eat His flesh and drink His blood means we are to believe in Him. He used the eating and drinking as a picture of believing in Him.

Doesn't this apply only to those who are the ones who have been "given" to the Son by the Father (v. 37)? Yes. But we don't have to know that we are given before we believe. We rather have to believe and then we may know that we are among the given.

-8-

From God's Word, the Bible...

Then Jesus spoke to them again, saying, "I am the light of the world. He who follows Me shall not walk in darkness, but have the light of life."

John 8:12

"I Am the Light of the World" (Jesus)

Darkness is everywhere in the first eleven verses of John 8. Sexual immorality is here. A woman has been caught in the act of adultery. But the hypocrisy of religious leaders is here also. Isn't it interesting that they have brought the woman to Jesus, but not the man? Hatred is here also. Because these religious leaders carried a smoldering hatred for Jesus, they are trying to set a trap for Him.

Against this backdrop of darkness, Jesus makes a cheering and staggering claim. He says: "I am the light of the world."

I think I would have enjoyed hearing Jesus speak those words. I know that I need light. I need it to guide me through this dark world. But my need goes beyond that. It's not just that I live in a dark world; it's rather that the darkness lives in me. And what I'm saying about myself is true of everyone else.

The Bible tells me that sin has done a real number on us. It has affected our minds, affections, and wills. It has so darkened our minds that we don't naturally understand the things of God (1 Cor. 2:14; 2 Cor. 4:3-4). It has so degraded our affections that we constantly place them on the low things of this earth instead of on the high things of God (Mark 7:21-23). It has even deadened our wills to the point that if we are left to ourselves we can't seek God or move toward Him (Rom. 3:11).

If the darkness is to be driven from us, our minds must be enlightened, our affections elevated, and our wills energized. Jesus is the light that we need. He enables us to understand, love, and choose Him and the salvation that He came to this earth to provide for sinners.

Jesus says He is the light of the world. We shouldn't take that to mean every single person in the world enjoys the salvation Jesus came to provide. Earlier in his Gospel, the Apostle John seems to suggest that. He calls Jesus "the true Light which gives light to every man who comes into the world" (John 1:9). Some have eagerly seized those words as proof that all will eventually be saved. But it's clear from the succeeding verses (vv. 10-11) that not all receive the light of Christ. What, then, is John 1:9 telling us? It's merely affirming that the light of Christ is there for all to see. But, sadly, the fact that the light is there for all to see doesn't mean all will see it.

The light we sinners need is shining in Christ, so let's heed His words: "He who follows Me shall not walk in darkness, but have the light of life."

To follow Christ is to believe in Him as our Savior and to obey Him as our Lord. It is to take His salvation by faith and to keep His commandments out of gratitude.

The Lord promises that those who follow Him will enjoy "the light of life." The Lord Jesus graciously drives the darkness out of all who believe in Him so that they pass from spiritual death into spiritual life. And the spiritual life that they receive from the Lord in this world will finally culminate in eternal life in heaven. There in heaven we will never again witness or experience the darkness created by sin.

As we journey through this dark world, let's sing these words from Philip P. Bliss:

> *The whole world was lost in the darkness of sin,*
> *The light of the world is Jesus!*
> *Like sunshine at noonday, His glory shone in;*
> *The light of the world is Jesus!*
>
> *No darkness have we who in Jesus abide;*
> *The light of the world is Jesus!*
> *We walk in the light when we follow our Guide!*
> *The Light of the world is Jesus!*
>
> *Ye dwellers in darkness with sin-blinded eyes,*
> *The Light of the world is Jesus!*
> *Go, wash at His bidding, and light will arise;*
> *The Light of the world is Jesus!*
>
> *No need of the sunlight in Heaven we're told;*
> *The Light of the world is Jesus!*
> *The Lamb is the Light in the city of gold,*
> *The Light of the world is Jesus!*
>
> Refrain:
> *Come to the light, 'tis shining for thee;*
> *Sweetly the light has dawned upon me;*
> *Once I was blind, now I can see:*
> *The Light of the world is Jesus!*

-9-

From God's Word, the Bible...

Then Jesus said to them again, "Most assuredly, I say to you, I am the door of the sheep. All who ever came before Me are thieves and robbers, but the sheep did not hear them. I am the door. If anyone enters by Me, he will be saved, and will go in and out and find pasture."

John 10:7-9

"I Am the Door" (Jesus)

I would like to have been there when Jesus said: "I am the door." I would have rejoiced in hearing that because I need a door. There's nothing that I need more. But I'm getting ahead of myself.

Two of Jesus' "I am" sayings are found in John 10. In the verses before us, Jesus claims to be "the door." Jesus also claims to be "the good shepherd" (vv. 11,14). He states each of these claims two times.

It's important to connect these two claims with the events reported in John 9. There we have Jesus healing a man born blind. Instead of rejoicing with this man, the religious leaders cast him out of the synagogue (vv. 22,34). Jesus began rebuking the religious leaders for their action in verse 41 of chapter 9, and He continues to do so in the first eighteen verses of chapter 10. The section beginning with 9:1 and ending with 10:39 is a unity and should be read as such.

By using the pictures of the door and the good shepherd,

Jesus is showing these religious leaders to be false and dangerous leaders. These men claimed to be the spiritual shepherds of the people, but they proved they weren't when they excommunicated the man healed of blindness.

Nothing is more important for our own spiritual wellbeing than being able to distinguish between true and false ministers. How are we to do this? The main thing to always keep in mind is this: the true ministry has a door in it.

The door to what? Doors to be doors must open so we can have access to something. By telling those religious leaders that He, Jesus, was the door, He was claiming to be the One who give access to something of tremendous importance—salvation from sin. Jesus says: "I am the door. If anyone enters by Me, he will be saved. . ." (v. 9).

The true minister is one who has used the door himself and is now pointing others to that door and urging them to use it. And the door is Jesus. So we can say the true minister is Christ-centered. He has received Jesus as his Lord and Savior, and he now preaches salvation through Christ to others.

On the other hand, the false minister doesn't use the door. He doesn't preach the coming and the dying of the Lord Jesus as the only means of salvation. He tries to get the sheep to follow him by approaching them in some way other than Christ. The final result of this approach is death.

But it's not enough to merely say the false minister is false. He is; but it's worse than that. The false minister is also a thief. By refusing to preach Christ as the way of salvation, he actually robs people of the very thing they so desperately need. He robs them of eternal salvation. Jesus gives spiritual life; the thief deprives people of the same (v. 10).

A couple of things should be very clear to us by now. One is that we should highly prize those ministries that have the door in them. We should prize Christ-centered ministers who faithfully set before us the saving work of the Lord Jesus. The other thing is that we should avoid those ministries and ministers that make no use of that door.

As Jesus pointed out, His people have a spiritual instinct that causes them to know when they are hearing the truth of God and when they aren't (vv. 4-5). But even God's people can be led astray. So we must be on guard. Listening to preachers is no small thing. Our spiritual wellbeing is at stake. So let's listen carefully and careful listening means listening for Christ, who is the door.

I thank God that, in my childhood years, I sat under the preaching of a man who put the door before me. He made me aware of the sinfulness that barred me from heaven, and when I began to feel the despair of being a sinner, my faithful pastor gloriously said: "Jesus is the door to heaven."

I heard that marvelous news and fled to Jesus. When I finally arrive in heaven, I want to find that Christ-preaching pastor, fall on his neck, and kiss him in gratitude for pointing me to the door.

-10-

From God's Word, the Bible...

"I am the good shepherd. The good shepherd gives His life for the sheep."

"I am the good shepherd; and I know My sheep, and am known by My own."

John 10:11,14

"I Am the Good Shepherd" (Jesus)

I need a shepherd. Just as I need a door, so I need a shepherd—a door to give me access to the kingdom of God and eternal life, and a shepherd to feed, guide, and protect me. Jesus is both the door and the shepherd that I need. Shortly after He healed a blind man in Jerusalem, Jesus claimed to be both.

There are false ministers and false ministries that have no door in them. They can't tell people how to enter heaven. And they, like the Pharisees of old, can't really shepherd people. In the previous reading, we looked at Jesus as the door. Now we look at Him as the shepherd.

The Lord Jesus is the good shepherd. No one can compare to Him. He uses ministers to shepherd His flock, but they are only under-shepherds. If they are what they ought to be, they are mindful that the sheep don't belong to them. The sheep belong to Christ, and they are to be shepherded with that in mind. They are to be shepherded in the way that the Lord wants it done.

How is it that the Lord Jesus has people as His sheep? The answer is that He laid down His life for them. John 10 reports Jesus saying four times that He was going to "lay down" His life for His sheep (vv. 11,15,17,18). That's what happened when Jesus was on the cross. He laid down His life for His sheep. His haters thought they were taking His life from Him. They were wrong. He didn't have to be on that cross. He was there because He chose to be. He was there to die for His sheep.

But why was it necessary for Him to die for His sheep? Could He not have had His flock apart from dying? No. His death was absolutely essential. His sheep would have died if He had not died in their stead.

All of us who are now the Lord's sheep used to be part of another flock. We come into this world as part of Satan's flock. Our sin has placed us in his flock. What a flock it is! The devil is the shepherd, and he holds us in his flock with the chain of sin. The only way out of his flock is for sin's penalty to be paid. If that penalty is paid, he has to let us go. And the penalty? It's is everlasting separation from God. The only way for us to pay that penalty ourselves is to be eternally separated from God. But, thank God, Jesus came to pay the penalty for His sheep. He came to experience, on the cross, an eternity of separation from God so His sheep could be released from the devil's flock and be in His flock.

The death of Jesus on the cross was substitutionary. He died in the place of His sheep. He received there what they would receive in eternity if He hadn't died in their place.

All those who trust in the Lord Jesus and what He did for them on the cross are now part of His flock. How can we be part of His flock if He died? The glorious answer is that He didn't stay dead. Yes, He died, but He also rose again. Right here in John 10, we have Him predicting His resurrection in these words: ". . . I lay down My life that I may take it again" (v. 17, see also v. 18).

Believers in Christ are the flock of a living shepherd. By His death on their behalf, He broke the chain of sin. By His resurrection from the grave, He proved that His death on the cross was pleasing to God and effective in securing our salvation.

Now it is our pleasure and delight to live each day as sheep in the flock of our living Savior. It is our delight to feed in the green pasture of His Word. It is our delight to walk peacefully along, knowing that we are free from sin's condemnation. It is our joy to know that even when we stray, He will not let us go but will seek us out and restore us (see Psalm 23).

While we weren't there to hear Jesus say: "I am the good shepherd," we rejoice with joy unspeakable in reading those precious words.

-11-

From God's Word, the Bible...

Jesus said to her, "I am the resurrection and the life. He who believes in Me, though he may die, he shall live. And whoever lives and believes in Me shall never die. Do you believe this?"

John 11:25-26

"I Am the Resurrection and the Life" (Jesus)

Siblings Mary, Martha, and Lazarus were dear to Jesus. But suddenly it didn't seem so. Lazarus had gotten sick, and Jesus hadn't come to heal him. Now he was dead—four days dead! The situation seemed to be utterly hopeless.

Mary and Martha were bewildered. Why hadn't Jesus come when they sent for Him? Why did Jesus let their brother die? They didn't know that Jesus had something in mind that would bring great glory to God and great comfort to them.

After Martha expressed her confidence that her brother would rise again "in the resurrection at the last day" (v. 24), Jesus made the fifth of His seven "I am" sayings. He said:

"I am the resurrection and the life." With those words, Jesus was essentially saying to Martha: "There's no need to wait for the resurrection at the end of time. I am the resurrection. The resurrection is here now."

And so it was! Jesus stepped up to the tomb of Lazarus and cried out: "Lazarus, come forth!" (v. 43). John, the author of this Gospel, states the result of that cry with marvelous brevity: "And he who had died came out. . ." (v. 44).

Lazarus was raised because Jesus was the resurrection and the life, just as He claimed.

That claim didn't pertain only to Lazarus. It also pertains to all believers in Christ, but—note it well—only to believers. It gives us consolation about death in all of its forms: physical, spiritual, and eternal.

Regarding physical death, Jesus says: "He who believes in Me, though he may die, he shall live" (v. 25).

Jesus raised Lazarus to give us a picture of the resurrection that awaits all believers. Death isn't final for God's people. The same Jesus who raised Lazarus will eventually come again, and when He comes He will raise the bodies of all His people, and refashion those bodies to conform to the resurrection body that He Himself has (Phil. 3:20-21).

Skeptics love to come up with scenarios that seemingly make the resurrection an impossibility. "What about that person who died thousands of years ago and has completely disintegrated? How could there possibly be a resurrection for him or her?" they ask. To that they add this: "What about that person who was blown to bits in war? Surely, there's nothing left to be raised."

Our answer is: "Look at Lazarus. His case seemed to be impossible, yet Jesus raised him."

Jesus' claim to be the resurrection and the life also pertains to the matter of spiritual death. This is our natural state. It means we are dead toward God. It's easy to miss this in Jesus' words, but it's there. In verse 26, He uses this phrase: "whoever lives and believes in Me."

The believer in Christ already has resurrection life. He is even now living in Christ. By the grace of God, he has been resurrected from spiritual death and made alive in Christ (Eph. 2:1,5-7).

That brings us to the third and final form of death—eternal death. Jesus also addressed that in His claim to be the resurrection and the life. He says those who believe in Him "shall never die" (v. 26).

The believer will never be separated from God in the world to come. He will never experience "the second death" (Rev. 20:14-15).

Unbelievers, who are already dead spiritually, have two more deaths to go—physical death and eternal death. With believers in Christ, it's different. Having been rescued from spiritual death, they only have one more death ahead of them. That is physical death, and those who are alive when Jesus comes won't even experience that (1 Thess. 4:17).

What a joy it is to be a Christian! We have already been made alive in Christ. We don't dread physical death because we know it won't be the final word for our bodies. And we never have to worry about eternal death because Christ has given us eternal life.

-12-

From God's Word, the Bible...

*Jesus said to him, "I am the way, the truth, and the life.
No one comes to the Father except through Me."*

John 14:6

"I Am the Way, the Truth, and the Life" (Jesus)

I am not ashamed to say that I want to go to heaven when I die. Nothing is more important to me than that. I am a mortal being passing with blinding speed through this world. Yes, I want to go to heaven!

If I'm to go to heaven, I must have a way. I don't need two, three or four ways. One will do. I won't reject that way merely because it's the only way. If there's only one way, I will rejoice in it and avail myself of it.

What a horrible thing it would be to know that heaven in all its glory is out there, but there's no way to get to it!

We don't have to face that horror because there is a way. The way is Jesus.

It's the night before his crucifixion, and Jesus is alone with His eleven disciples (Judas already having departed). These disciples are filled with sorrow because they now know full well that Jesus will soon depart from them.

Their sorrow so touched the heart of Jesus that He offered one consolation after another to them. One of those consolations was heaven, which Jesus refers to as His Father's "house" (v. 1).

Furthermore, Jesus assured the disciples that they knew the "where" and the "way" (v. 4). They knew where He was going, and they knew the way to get there. Thomas begged to differ, saying: "Lord, we do not know where You are going, and how can we know the way?" (v. 5).

It was at that point that Jesus gave the sixth of His seven "I am" sayings: "I am the way, the truth, and the life" (v. 6).

Wonderful news! There is a way to get to heaven, and that way is Jesus!

How is it that Jesus is the way to heaven? What is there about Him that makes Him the way? The answer is His death on the cross. Let's never forget that everything we read in John 14 is set in the context of the cross.

What is so special about Jesus' death on the cross? In dying there, Jesus received the penalty for sin. It is our sin that blocks our entrance into heaven. God won't allow sinners to enter there in their sin. Their sin must be removed, and the only way sin can be removed is for its penalty to be paid. Jesus went to the cross to pay that penalty. He went there to receive the wrath of God in the place of sinners. Since Jesus paid the penalty for sin, it can no longer bar us from heaven. By His death on the cross, Jesus took sin out of the way, and He became the way.

It's very important that we understand that Jesus wasn't simply claiming to be a way to heaven. He says He is "the way." Jesus is the only way to heaven because He is the only one who could deal with the sin that keeps us out of heaven.

In addition to claiming to be the way, Jesus claims to be the "the truth and the life." I suggest that those terms are subsidiary to the way. It is "the way" that predominates in this sentence. "The truth" and "the life" are themselves part of Jesus being the way.

What does it mean for Jesus to be the truth? It means that He reveals to us every truth that pertains to salvation. He shows us the sin that keeps us from heaven, and the cross that removes the sin.

What does it mean for Jesus to be the life? The Bible tells us that we are "dead in trespasses and sins" (Eph. 2:1). It doesn't help a dead person to have a way to heaven put before him. He can't walk it. When Jesus called Himself "the life," He was affirming that He not only shows sinners the way to heaven but also gives them the ability to walk that way.

All of salvation is God's grace. It is God's grace that there is a way to heaven. It is God's grace that shows us the way. And it is God's grace that enables us to walk the way. So, to say it again, the way is Jesus.

What a cheering word this was for the eleven disciples who heard it on the night before the Lord Jesus was crucified! It is no less cheering as we read today what He said then. Are you trusting in Christ as the Way to heaven, and are you on your way there?

-13-

From God's Word, the Bible...

"I am the true vine, and My Father is the vinedresser."

"I am the vine, you are the branches. He who abides in Me, and I in him, bears much fruit; for without Me you can do nothing."

John 15:1, 5

"I Am the Vine" (Jesus)

God made us to bear fruit for Him. How do we live up to that purpose? How do we bear fruit for God? We do so by obeying His commandments. In keeping those commandments, we reflect His image and we bring honor to His name.

Sin makes us unfruitful. It causes us to come short of the purpose for which God made us. Sin is refusing to obey God's commandments. Every time we refuse to obey, we fail to reflect God's image and to live for His glory. We might say sin makes all of us unfruitful vines.

God could have given up on us. He could have said: "I will never get any fruit from those sinful people." He could have just plowed us under.

But God took another approach. He sent His Son, Jesus, to be "the true vine" (v. 1). We are all dead vines, bearing no fruit for God because of our sin. But all is not lost. We can still bear fruit for God, not as vines in and of ourselves, but by being connected to the Lord Jesus, who is the true vine. If we abide in Jesus, we shall bear "much fruit" (v. 5).

By calling Himself the "true vine," Jesus was affirming that He is the only vine that works in this matter of bearing fruit for God. Merely belonging to a church won't work. That is a false vine. Performing a few good works here and there won't work. That is another false vine. No one will ever be able to produce the fruit that God demands and finally enter into heaven, except through the Lord Jesus Christ. Apart from Him, we can do nothing (v. 5).

So, the most urgent matter in this life is to make sure we are connected to the vine, that is, to make sure we are connected to Christ. This takes place by God graciously working in us and bringing us to faith. By grace through faith we are saved (Eph. 2:8-9).

Jesus mentions a dreadful possibility in regard to the issue of being connected with Him. It is having the appearance of being connected without actually being connected (v. 6). Judas Iscariot would be the prime example of this. Everyone would have said that he was truly connected to Christ, but he wasn't.

Look at what happens to those who aren't truly in Christ. They are taken away (v. 2), "cast out" (v. 6), "withered" (v. 6) and "burned" (v. 6).

How few these days seems to realize the tremendous weight of these words! Let's make sure we allow them to sink in. A great day of taking away is coming for all those who aren't in Christ (Matt. 7:21-23).

How do we know that we are truly connected to Christ? We must ask ourselves two questions. The first is this: Am I producing fruit? Am I obeying the Lord's commandments and living for His glory? Those who don't produce fruit, no matter what they profess, aren't vitally connected to the vine, which is Jesus.

All Christians produce fruit, but not all are equally fruitful. We've all noticed this. Some Christians grow robust and strong, while others are stunted. The Lord wants all of us to reach the level of "much fruit." To achieve that end, He resorts to that measure all gardeners are familiar with—pruning. One of His sharp pruning devices is His Word. He uses it to cut away things that are hindering our spiritual growth and productivity (Heb. 4:12). God may also use chastisement to the same end.

God's pruning devices can be painful, but they produce positive results. They yield the positive fruit of righteousness, and they prove to us that we are indeed connected to Christ (Heb. 12:3-11).

The second question we must ask ourselves is this: Am I abiding in Christ? To abide in the Lord means we continue with Him. We continue believing, obeying, and serving. Continuance—endurance—is ever the mark of reality (John 8:31; 1 John 2:24; 2 John 9). If we don't continue in the faith, it's because we never really possessed it (1 John 2:19).

God says to me: "You are a worthless, fruitless, dead vine, but I am going to get fruit from you by connecting you to a living, fruitful vine." I think I would like to have been there to hear Jesus say: "I am the vine."

-14-

From God's Word, the Bible...

Jesus spoke these words, lifted up His eyes to heaven, and said:
"Father, the hour has come. Glorify Your Son,
that Your Son also may glorify You. . . ."

John 17:1

Jesus Speaks to His Father

The seventeenth chapter of John records a prayer that Jesus prayed the night before He was crucified. This wasn't the prayer that He offered in Gethsemane. The opening words of John 18 indicate that Jesus prayed this prayer while He and His eleven true disciples were still in the Upper Room. So all of those disciples heard the prayer. Jesus had given them many words of comfort and encouragement prior to this prayer, but they probably found it to be more comforting than anything else He said.

These men had heard Jesus preach and teach on many occasions. Blessed men were they! On this night they were privileged to hear Him offer the most wonderful prayer ever prayed. I'm sure these disciples had heard Jesus pray on numerous occasions, but this prayer—there was none like it!

The prayer falls into three easily discernible parts. First, *Jesus prayed that His Father would be glorified* (vv. 1-5).

At first glance, it doesn't seem so because Jesus begins:

"Father, the hour has come. Glorify Your Son. . ." (v. 1).

The reason Jesus began that way quickly becomes apparent. It was necessary for Jesus to be glorified so He could glorify the Father.

The word "glorify" means "to honor" or "to magnify." The consuming priority of Jesus' life was to bring honor to His Father (John 7:18; 8:50; 12:27-28; 13:31-32).

To honor His Father meant that Jesus would have to finish the work the Father had sent Him to do. That was the work of the cross by which He would secure the gift of eternal life for all those who were "given" to Him by the Father (v. 2). Before the world began, the Father gave Jesus to us, and He gave all believers to the Lord Jesus. What a wonderful double gift!

Let's not miss this important detail in this part of Jesus' prayer—He speaks of the work on the cross as being already finished (v. 4). He is yet to be crucified, but He speaks as if He had already been crucified. This shows us that there was no uncertainty about whether Jesus would complete the work of redemption.

Jesus also prayed for the eleven disciples who were with Him (vv. 6-19). He prayed that they be kept or protected (vv.11,15), that they be united (v.11), that they experience His joy (v.13), and that they be sanctified or separated from the world (v.17).

His disciples would need protection because the world would hate them (v. 14). There's no surprise here because the hating world is under the control of "the evil one" (v.15).

Jesus may have prayed for His disciples to be united for this very reason—the evil one who inspires the hatred of the world works feverishly to alienate believers from each other. And He may have prayed for them to know His joy to sustain them in a world that could wring the joy out of them.

His disciples would need to be sanctified or set apart

because this evil world carries a strange attraction for believers and has the power to draw them away from faithfulness to Christ. If believers are to maintain purity in such a world, they must immerse themselves in "the truth" (v.19), that is, the Word of God.

Finally, *Jesus prayed for His future disciples* (vv. 20-24). He first asked that they also be united (v. 21). We shouldn't think He was speaking in terms of mere organizational unity. It was spiritual unity that He had in mind. We know all too well that people who belong to one church don't necessarily have unity. On the other hand, Christians who belong to different denominations don't necessarily find themselves divided. There is a kinship among all true Christians, regardless of their denominational distinctions.

Jesus also prayed that His future disciples would share His glory. This petition will finally be fulfilled when we get to heaven.

Jesus concluded his prayer by resolving to declare the Father's name (vv. 25-26). He had, of course, declared it to the disciples during His time with them, and He was determined to continue to declare it. By His death on the cross, His resurrection, His post-resurrection appearances, His ascension, and His gift of the Holy Spirit to his church, the Lord Jesus abundantly kept this resolve.

The eleven men who heard that prayer had to know that they were listening to words "fitly spoken" and must have rejoiced in having such a Savior.

-15-

From God's Word, the Bible...

Then Jesus said, "Father, forgive them,
for they do not know what they do."
And they divided His garments and cast lots.

Luke 23:34

"Father, Forgive Them..." (Jesus)

The first words from Jesus' lips after He was nailed to cross were these: "Father, forgive them, for they do not know what they do."

I know I shouldn't be surprised to read that Jesus' first words from the cross came in the form of a prayer. Jesus was a man of prayer, and Luke loved to emphasize this. He informs us that Jesus prayed at His baptism (3:21), before selecting His disciples (6:12), on the Mount of Transfiguration (9:28-29), and on the night before He was crucified (22:41,44). Luke also tells us that Jesus "often withdrew into the wilderness and prayed" (5:16). In addition to praying Himself, Jesus taught His disciples that "men always ought to pray and not lose heart" (18:1).

But I'm still somewhat surprised to read that Jesus prayed. I think my surprise is due to Luke writing the word "Then." "Then Jesus said, 'Father, forgive them. . . .'"

There's a ton of marvel in that "Then." By using it Luke

is reminding us of all that had happened to Jesus in the hours preceding His crucifixion. Taken into custody in the middle of the night to endure legal proceedings that were themselves illegal! Mocked, ridiculed and spat on! Scourged until the flesh of His back was a mass of bloody ribbons! Crowned with a crown of thorns! Paraded through the streets of Jerusalem and out to Golgotha! Nailed to the cross! Think about all of it, and then think about it again, and then marvel at Luke's "Then." It captures all of these things. After all the humiliation, the pain, and the ridicule, Jesus prays!

Part of the marvel of Luke's "Then" is that Jesus addresses God as "Father." Although His Father could have saved Him from the cross, the Lord Jesus isn't angry. There's love and trust in His word, "Father." We need to learn from Jesus to continue to love and trust God when our circumstances rise up against us, saying with Edward Mote:

> *When darkness seems to hide His face,*
> *I rest on His unchanging grace.*
> *When all around my soul gives way*
> *He then is all my hope and stay.*

But now we move from "Then" to "them." Jesus prays: "Father, forgive them. . . ." In the midst of His excruciating pain, Jesus is thinking about His Father and about others. He had taught that love for God and love for others are the greatest of the commandments, and He is practicing those commandments even as He dies.

But for whom is He praying when He uses the word "them?" The Jewish leaders who were behind His crucifixion? The Roman soldiers who nailed Him to the cross? The multitude that stood staring at Him?

Charles Spurgeon says:

I love this prayer . . . because of the indistinctness of it. . . . Now into that pronoun "them" I feel that I can crawl. Can you get in there? Oh, by a humble faith appropriate the cross of Christ by trusting in it: and get into that big little word "them"! It seems like a chariot of mercy that has come down to earth, into which a man may step and it shall bear him up to heaven.[2]

A young fellow who was angry with his mother included in his bedtime prayer a reference to everyone in the family except her. When he crawled into bed, he looked at her and said: "I suppose you noticed you were not in it."

How very thankful we should be, as Spurgeon pointed out, that there's room in Jesus' "them" for all who want God's forgiveness! Let's not debate the word "them," but rather do as Spurgeon urged and "crawl" in there.

Jesus' prayer from the cross is an apple of gold. Have you seen the marvel of it? Avis B. Christiansen saw it and wrote:

> *"Father, forgive them!" thus did He pray,*
> *E'en while His life blood flowed fast away;*
> *Praying for sinners while in such woe—*
> *No one but Jesus ever loved so.*
>
> *Blessed Redeemer! Precious Redeemer!*
> *Seems now I see Him on Calvary's tree;*
> *Wounded and bleeding, for sinners pleading,*
> *Blind and unheeding—dying for me!*

---

[2] Charles Spurgeon, *Metropolitan Tabernacle Pulpit*, Pilgrim Publications, Pasadena, TX, no date, vol. 38, p. 318.

-16-

From God's Word, the Bible...

*And Jesus said to him, "Assuredly, I say to you,
today you will be with Me in Paradise."*

Luke 23:43

"Today, You Will Be with Me in Paradise" (Jesus)

The Lord Jesus was hanging on a cross between two common criminals, and the religious leaders of the Jews were filled with glee. To them it was the ultimate proof that He was a fraud. He wouldn't have been there between two thieves if He really was the Messiah. Little did they realize that what they regarded as proof of their position was just the opposite. The prophet Isaiah had said that in His death the Messiah would be "numbered with the transgressors" (Isa. 53:12).

One of these two thieves, after initially joining in the mockery that was being heaped on Jesus, suddenly stopped and said to Him: "Lord, remember me when You come into Your kingdom."

Jesus answered that prayer by assuring the man that the two of them would be together that day in Paradise. So the first time Jesus spoke from the cross was to pray. The second time He spoke was to answer prayer.

Let's think about this thief: he was, by his own admission, a sinful man (v. 41). The Lord Jesus was dying the death of a criminal, but He was innocent. This man was dying the death of a criminal because he was a criminal.

To state the obvious, this thief was also a dying man. His wasted life was quickly drawing to a close. His blood was flowing out of his tortured body and falling to the ground. Hell's mouth was opening wide to receive his soul.

Sinful and dying! That sounds just like us! We are all sinners, and we are all dying. It's important for us to identify with this thief because it is only as we do that we are in the position to receive the thrilling assurances that he received.

What were those assurances? One was that he, the thief, was right about Jesus. He called Him "Lord," and Jesus didn't correct or rebuke him. Jesus accepted the title and responded to this man in the fashion of being Lord. It was God's grace that enabled this man to see the truth about Jesus because "no one can say that Jesus is Lord except by the Holy Spirit" (1 Cor. 12:3).

Another assurance that the thief received was that he was right to believe in heaven. Jesus didn't say to him: "You're wrong about this business of Me coming into My kingdom. There's no such place as heaven. You might as well accept the fact that when people die, they're dead. That's all there is to it."

The truth is that heaven is a present reality for those who believe in Christ. The Lord Jesus said, "Today," to this man. That means that his soul would go to heaven as soon as he died. The Apostle Paul assures us that as soon as we are absent from the body, we are present with the Lord (2 Cor. 5:6-8).

Yet another assurance was that Jesus does indeed possess the authority to open heaven's door. Jesus didn't say to him: "You're talking to the wrong person. I'm not the way to heaven." Instead He promised that this man would enter heaven that very day.

This thief had been wrong all of his life, but suddenly "the wrong man" had become "the right man." He came to the right person, Jesus, about the right matter, heaven, and he came in the right way, humbly casting himself on the Lord for mercy.

The words of Jesus to this dying thief were an apple of gold. Fitly spoken words were they! How thankful we should be that they are reported to us in Scripture! They assure us that we will have a home in heaven if we will come to Jesus. No matter how sinful we have been, we can be forgiven.

But we must never think of this one thief without thinking of the other. This man refused to cast himself upon the mercy of the Lord. So he died without salvation, and without salvation he couldn't enter heaven. It wasn't an accident that Jesus' cross was placed between these two thieves. He is the great divider of men. Those who receive Him are saved. Those who reject Him are lost. On which side of the Lord Jesus are you?

-17-

From God's Word, the Bible...

When Jesus therefore saw His mother, and the disciple whom He loved standing by, He said to His mother, "Woman, behold your son!" Then He said to the disciple, "Behold your mother!" And from that hour that disciple took her to his own home.

John 19:26-27

"Woman, Behold Your Son" (Jesus)

All of Jesus' disciples had fled from Him in the hours preceding His crucifixion, but John, the author of this Gospel, had thought better of his cowardice, and had taken his place at the foot of Jesus' cross. We know he was there because he identifies himself as "the disciple whom Jesus loved."

By using that title for himself, John was able to avoid using his name again and again in this Gospel. It was his way of being modest. But it was also more than that. The glory of John's life lay in knowing that he was loved by the Lord Jesus. John didn't glory in his love for Christ. It was far too weak and faltering for that. But the love of the Lord for him, ah, that was something in which to glory. Reflecting on that love must have been the thing that drew him back to his rightful place.

John wasn't alone at the foot of the cross. Jesus' mother, Mary, was there with him, and Jesus, in the anguish of suffering, could see them there. That prompted Him to speak His third word from the cross. A double word it was—spoken first to Mary and then to John. "Woman, behold your son!" and then, "Behold your mother!"

Jesus' meaning was clear. He was committing the care of His mother to John. In doing so, He was manifesting tender concern for one who was in great need. The future must have looked very bleak to Mary. What was to become of her? Jesus' words gave the answer, and those words found their mark because we read that John "from that hour" took Mary "to his own home" (v. 27).

So, Jesus wasn't so occupied with His own needs that He neglected the needs of His mother. Others had always been at the forefront of Jesus' life, and they were again in His death. His first three words from the cross were spoken on behalf of others. This isn't surprising. His first priority was God; His second was others.

The Lord Jesus is still concerned about the needs of others today. So we can and should bring our needs to Him. In heaven as our High Priest, He sympathizes with us in all of our cares (Heb. 4:15).

And Jesus' concern for others teaches us who follow Him to be concerned about others as well. Have we learned this lesson, or have we fallen prey to the self-centeredness that is so prevalent these days?

In committing His mother to John's care, Jesus was showing His concern for what was left of her life in this world. But He didn't allow that issue, important as it was, to crowd out a larger issue—the life beyond this world.

This comes out in a couple of ways. First, the fact that Jesus was concerned about Mary and her physical needs didn't bring Him down from the cross. He didn't have to stay on the cross. He could have laid aside the work He was doing there. He could have put Mary's physical needs above the work of redemption, but He didn't. He gave priority to the matter of opening the door of heaven to all who savingly believe in Him.

Many seem to only be interested in the Jesus of physical needs, wanting Him to be exclusively concerned about them in the here and now. They want to accept the lesser gift of His care for the problems of this life, while they reject the greater gift of eternal life. The tragedy is that they can have both.

The second indication that Jesus gave priority to the next life is shown in the way that He addressed Mary. He called her "Woman." Some are disturbed by this because they think Jesus was being rude to His mother. Nothing could be farther from the truth. Jesus addressed Mary as "Woman," not to be rude, but rather to underscore a most vital truth, namely, that their relationship was now forever changed. Mary was now a simple believer in her Lord—the One who had purchased her salvation by dying on the cross.

Jesus created a new family with His words to Mary and John. Through His death, Jesus creates a new family for all those who believe—the family of God. What a blessing that is!

-18-

From God's Word, the Bible...

Now from the sixth hour until the ninth hour there was darkness over all the land. And about the ninth hour Jesus cried out with a loud voice, saying, "Eli, Eli, lama sabachthani?" that is, "My God, My God, why have You forsaken Me?"

Matthew 27:45-46

"My God, My God, Why Have You Forsaken Me?" (Jesus)

Jesus was nailed to the cross at nine in the morning. He died at three in the afternoon. The first three of His seven words from the cross were spoken during His first three hours on the cross. The last four were spoken in quick succession just before He died.

From noon to three, Jesus said nothing. These were the hours when darkness fell over the land, the hours at which the sun normally shines most brightly. After those three long hours, Jesus cried: "My God, My God, why have You forsaken Me?"

This was His fourth word, with three on each side of it. It was the center word. That is strikingly appropriate because it brings us to the very center of the meaning of Jesus' death. It is Jesus' own explanation of those hours of darkness. They were hours in which God withdrew from Him.

Why did the Father withdraw from Jesus? If we are to understand this amazing thing, we must address the problem the cross was designed to deal with—the problem created by man's sinfulness and God's holiness.

What is sin? It is refusing to live according to God's commandments. God cannot and will not regard sin as a trifling matter. Why does God take sin so seriously? He is holy, and His holy nature requires Him to judge sin. For God to ignore sin or refuse to punish it would make Him guilty of sin Himself.

But it's not enough to say God is holy. He is. But He is also gracious. And while His holiness demands that He judge sinners by forever separating them from Himself, His grace demands that He forgive sinners.

How could the holy God both punish sinners and let them go free? How could He both satisfy the demands of His justice and the demands of His grace when those demands seemed to be conflicting and contradictory? The answer is the cross of Christ. The Apostle Paul says that Jesus was "made" sin on the cross (2 Cor. 5:21). The sins of others were laid on Him.

For God to count Jesus as guilty of the sins of others required Him, God, to forsake Jesus because the penalty for sin is God-forsakenness (2 Thess. 1:9). If God had refused to truly forsake Jesus, He could not have counted Him the substitute for sinners. That forsaking had to take place!

Some people argue that God did not really forsake Jesus on the cross. It was rather a matter of Jesus only feeling that He was forsaken. But if that had not been a true forsaking, there would have been no atonement for sinners.

The glory of it all is that God only requires that the penalty for sin be paid once. If Jesus paid it, there is no penalty left for all those who take refuge in Jesus through faith. In other words, God cannot punish Jesus for my sins and then proceed to punish me as well. That would be unjust! If Jesus bore my God-forsakenness on the cross, there is, therefore, no such forsakenness for me to bear. The cross was, then, God's way of satisfying both the demands of His justice and His grace. Justice looked upon the cross that day and said: "I'm satisfied. The penalty of God-forsakenness against sinners has been carried out."

And grace looked upon that same cross and said: "I'm satisfied. Since Jesus bore the penalty of God-forsakenness for all who believe, they will never have to bear it themselves and can, therefore, be forgiven."

If someone asks how Jesus could bear in a short period of time an eternity's worth of wrath, we must admit that we are out of our element. We can only say that as God in human flesh, Jesus had the capacity to bear an infinite measure of wrath in a finite length of time.

God will either find our sins on Jesus or on us. If He finds them on Jesus, we will never have to endure their penalty, but if He finds them on us, we must hear from God those tragic words: "Depart from Me" (Matt. 7:23; 25:41).

We can read Jesus' cry to the Father and say: "Jesus forsaken by His Father! What a horrible thing!" Yes, it was. But we can also read those same words and say: "In that cry lies my salvation! What a wonderful thing!"

-19-

From God's Word, the Bible...

After this, Jesus, knowing that all things were now accomplished, that the Scripture might be fulfilled, said, "I thirst!" Now a vessel full of sour wine was sitting there; and they filled a sponge with sour wine, put it on hyssop, and put it to His mouth.

John 19:28-29

"I Thirst"
(Jesus)

We have no trouble seeing the significance of the first four statements that Jesus made from the cross. But this statement! What are we to make of it?

It's no surprise that Jesus was thirsty. Many hours had probably elapsed without Him having taken a sip of water. The question is rather why John thought it important to report this cry. There would seem to be no great significance in a dying man thirsting and asking for a drink.

The answer, I think, is that John, prompted by the Holy Spirit, saw truths of great importance in Jesus' thirst. He, John, understood that there was more to Jesus' thirst than mere thirst. There was more to it than what lies on the surface. John wanted us to know about Jesus' thirst so we would know the truth about Jesus. And what is that truth? It is that Jesus was fully God and fully man.

Why is this important? Why do we need to know that Jesus was the God-man? We need to understand that Jesus came to this earth and went to that cross to serve as the mediator between God and sinful men and women. A mediator is one who steps between parties in conflict and makes peace between them.

For Jesus to be the mediator between God and people, He had to represent each. To represent God, He had to be God. There was no problem there. He was already God. He had always been God. But He also had to represent men. To do that, He had to do that which we celebrate at Christmas— He had to take our humanity. That doesn't mean that He laid aside His deity. It rather means that He added our humanity to His deity. In doing that, He became the God-man and was able to represent both God and men.

Let's get back to the matter of Jesus' thirst. How did it show that Jesus was God? The answer is that it was a fulfillment of prophecy (Ps. 69:21).

We must not think that Jesus was a mere helpless victim when He died on the cross. We can go so far as to say that Jesus was in control of His own crucifixion. He was keeping a mental checklist of all the prophecies that His crucifixion had to fulfill, and crying "I thirst" was one of them.

Very few realize the immense importance of Jesus fulfilling prophecies. One author calculated the probability of one man fulfilling forty-eight prophecies of the Old Testament to a blindfolded man picking a marked electron out of a one-inch line of electrons. It would take nineteen million years just to count those electrons! Supposing the blindfolded man could actually pick up an electron, what chance would he have of getting the one that was marked? It's the same probability of one man fulfilling forty-eight Old Testament prophecies. And Jesus fulfilled, not 48, but 325!

Yes, the thirst of Jesus shows us that He was God, but it also shows us that He was fully man. "I thirst," is a human cry. Thirst means we have a need, and God doesn't need anything. God doesn't get thirsty.

The thirst of Jesus, if we will let it, will convince us that Jesus' humanity was real. It will persuade us to not downplay His humanity. Some have a tendency to do this. They seem to think that it is a disservice to Jesus to emphasize His humanity. They give the impression that Jesus' humanity was only a pretend humanity.

We must never minimize the humanity of Christ for this reason—there would be no salvation without it. It was humanity that sinned against God, and God's justice demanded that humanity pay the penalty for sin. For Jesus to pay that penalty on our behalf, He had to be one of us.

The thirst of Jesus takes us to the very heart of our salvation because it takes us to the true identity of the One who came to provide that salvation. Jesus thirsted on the cross as the God-man so we could both thirst for salvation and have that thirst quenched:

> *I heard the voice of Jesus say,*
> *"Behold, I freely give*
> *The living water; thirsty one,*
> *stoop down and drink, and live"*
> *I came to Jesus, and I drank*
> *Of that life-giving stream;*
> *My thirst was quenched, my soul revived,*
> *And now I live in Him.*
> (Horatius Bonar)

-20-

From God's Word, the Bible...

So when Jesus had received the sour wine, He said, "It is finished!"
And bowing His head, He gave up His spirit.

John 19:30

"It Is Finished!" (Jesus)

It's easy to think of lots of things that we are glad to have out of the way. Boring meetings, car trouble, sickness and socializing with difficult, obnoxious people—all fall into that category. When we come to the end of such things, we might well exclaim, "I'm glad that's over!"

We might think that the sixth word Jesus spoke from the cross belongs in the category of rejoicing to have reached the end of something unpleasant. Crucifixion was such an incredibly horrid and agonizing thing, we can well imagine crucified men finally gasping: "It's finally over!"

But that's not what Jesus was saying when He cried, "It is finished!" He wasn't speaking as a tortured man who was glad to see His suffering come to an end. There's a huge difference between ending something and accomplishing something. With His cry, Jesus wasn't merely saying that He was ending something. He was saying that He had accomplished something.

What is the "it" to which Jesus referred? It was the "it" which brought Him to this world. What was that "it"? Jesus Himself stated it several times. In Luke 19:10, we find Him saying: "The Son of Man has come to seek and to save that which was lost."

In Mark 10:45, He says: ". . . the Son of Man did not come to be served but to serve, and to give His life a ransom for many."

In John 3:17, He says: "For God did not send His Son into the world to condemn the world, but that the world through Him might be saved."

These are just three of the many verses in which Jesus talks about the "it" that brought Him to earth. These verses tell us that Jesus came to provide salvation for sinners, and that He had to die in their stead in order to provide it.

The "it" to which Jesus was referring when He died was the "it" of our salvation. As we noted in a previous reading, "it" is the "it" of Psalm 40:7 (and Hebrews 10:7) when Jesus said to God the Father:

"Behold, I come;
In the scroll of the Book, it is written of me."

Do you see the "it" in those words? When Jesus came to this earth, He told the Father that He was coming to do the "it" that He and the Father had planned before the world began—the salvation for sinners. With the cry, "It is finished!" Jesus was affirming that He had accomplished that which He, the Father, and the Holy Spirit had planned. He wasn't speaking as a victim, but rather as a victor who had crossed the finish line.

What did finishing this "it" require of Jesus? In other words, what exactly did Jesus have to do to accomplish our salvation? What was necessary to save sinners from sin?

First, Jesus had to live a sinless life, that is, a life of perfect obedience to God. This was God's requirement from the very beginning. If Adam and Eve had perfectly obeyed the commandment God gave them in Eden, they would have received the gift of eternal life. God has never changed the condition for receiving that life. He still demands perfect obedience from us. We can't meet this demand, but Jesus met it. He lived the sinless life that God requires, and God puts the righteousness of Christ to the account of all who come to Christ. He counts Christ's righteousness as though it were their righteousness.

But what about our sins? Jesus went to the cross, not to die as others do, but rather to die a special death. He went there to receive the wrath that our sins deserve.

Here is Christianity in a nutshell: Jesus got my sins on the cross, and I get His righteousness.

When Jesus cried, "It is finished!" He was affirming that He had completed the work of salvation for all who would believe in Him. He had met all the requirements for saving sinners.

Perhaps someone will ask about the resurrection of Jesus. Why did Jesus claim that everything was finished before His resurrection? The answer is that He had done all that He came to do. It was the Father's work to raise Him from the dead (Acts 2:42; 17:31).

We should rejoice over Jesus' cry. We couldn't be saved without it. It is an apple of gold in a setting of silver.

-21-

From God's Word, the Bible...

And when Jesus had cried out with a loud voice, He said, "Father, 'into Your hands I commit My spirit.'" Having said this, He breathed His last.

Luke 23:46

"Father, into Your Hands, I Commit My Spirit" (Jesus)

The last words spoken from the cross reveal that Jesus died with great confidence and without fear and trembling. He spoke of death in terms of placing Himself in His Father's hands. His words draw the picture of someone depositing something for safe keeping with one who is unquestionably trustworthy.

Would we know how to die? We should look to the Lord Jesus. His last words from the cross show us that *we can die well if we die knowing God is our heavenly Father.*

Of course, we can't have God as our Father in exactly the same way that Jesus did. Jesus was—and is—the eternal Son of God. But we can still have God as our Father. This is the glory of the Christian message. Each of us can know God through the redeeming work of Christ.

Some argue that God is already the Father of all, but a quick glance at Scripture reveals that this is not true. In John 1:12, we read of Jesus: "But as many as received Him, to them He gave the right to become children of God, even those who believe in His name."

Who can be called the children of God? Is it everyone without exception? No. This verse says that only those who believe in Christ are the children of God. Those who reject Christ don't have God as their Father (John 8:42).

We also learn from Jesus' last words that *we can die well if we die knowing that our souls will go immediately into the hands of our heavenly Father.*

Jesus had been in the hands of wicked people (Matt. 17:22-23; 26:45). As He died, He knew that was no longer the case. Human hands had done all that they could do to Him, and now He could commit Himself into His Father's hands.

Jesus knew His soul was going to be received by the Father at the very moment of His death. His body, of course, would be placed in a tomb and would be resurrected on the third day. At the time of His resurrection, His soul and body would be reunited. But His soul was safe in the Father's hands while His body was entombed.

It's exactly the same with each person who knows God. At the point of death, his soul goes immediately into God's presence and remains there until his body is raised from the grave. At that time, his soul and body will be joined together again and will live forever with the Lord (1 Thess. 4:13-18).

For the Christian, this takes the sting out of death. Tell him that he is about to die, and he will rejoice in knowing that to be absent from the body is to be present with the Lord (2 Cor. 5:6-8). The unbeliever doesn't have this comfort.

There's another set of hands ready to receive him at the moment of death.

We should also learn from Jesus' dying words that *we can die well if we die knowing our work is done*.

Jesus spoke His last word from the cross immediately after He cried: "It is finished!" The Lord Jesus came into this world with a mission that was clearly laid out for Him by His Father. Jesus carefully and diligently followed that plan. He was able to say: "For I have come down from heaven, not to do My own will, but the will of Him who sent Me" (John 6:38).

God also has a plan for all those who belong to Christ. He has given them a work to do even as He gave Jesus work to do. We are called to "proclaim the praises" of God who has called us "out of darkness into His marvelous light" (1 Peter 2:9). We're to be fulfilling this purpose in our families, on our jobs and in our churches and communities. Wherever we go and whatever we do, we are to be conscious that we belong to God and that we are to live for God.

Because we are fallible and frail, we cannot perfectly fulfill our purpose as the Lord Jesus did His, but we can be striving to do better all the time, knowing as we strive that death will be far more comfortable for those that so strive.

Jesus' dying word was a fitly spoken word. We should make Him our example by seeking to live as He lived and to die as He died.

-22-

From God's Word, the Bible...

So when the centurion and those with him, who were guarding Jesus, saw the earthquake and the things that had happened, they feared greatly, saying, "Truly this was the Son of God!"

Matthew 27:54

A Centurion Speaks about Jesus

The Gospels report several impressive confessions of faith. There's one from John the Baptist (John 1:29) and one from Nathanael (John 1:49). There are two from Simon Peter (Matt. 16:16; John 6:68-69). To these we can add the confessions of all Jesus' disciples (Matt. 14:33), that of Martha (John 11:27), and that of Thomas (John 20:28).

I think that the most impressive of all the confessions presented in the Gospels came from a man who stood at the foot of Jesus' cross. I'm referring to the Roman centurion.

He certainly doesn't qualify as one from whom we would expect an awestruck confession of faith in Jesus. It's probably safe to assume that this man had supervised many crucifixions. If so, he would have been a very hardened man. Furthermore, since the Romans employed crucifixion for very bad men, this centurion wouldn't have been inclined to conclude that one of them was the Son of God. But that's exactly what he concluded about Jesus.

How long had this man been in direct contact with Jesus? We can't say. It's likely that he was present when the soldiers in his command mocked and scourged Jesus. It's likely that he saw them press their cruel crown of thorns upon His head. He was certainly present when his soldiers prodded Jesus through the streets of Jerusalem and out to Golgotha. He stood watching as his men nailed Jesus to the cross, hoisted it in the air, and dropped it in the ground. He heard the insults and ridicule that were heaped on Jesus by his own soldiers, the religious leaders of the Jews, the two men who were crucified with Jesus, and those who were only passing by. He may have even participated in the mockery himself.

The Bible doesn't tell us that this man made his confession before Jesus was crucified or while He was being crucified. His confession came when Jesus was dead. So, the centurion had to see evidence along the way that Jesus was far more than an ordinary man.

The way Jesus suffered must have made an impression on him. It was obvious that Jesus was different from other men.

And the first words Jesus spoke from the cross asked God to forgive those who were crucifying Him (Luke 23:34). The centurion had never heard anything like that. The men he had seen crucified usually cursed those who were crucifying them.

Jesus said to one of the two thieves who were being crucified with Him: "Assuredly, I say to you, today you will be with Me in Paradise" (Luke 23:43). The centurion must have heard that and asked himself: "Who is this that expresses concern for another while He is enduring such agony? And how can He assure a thief that he will go to heaven?"

The evidence for Jesus was piling up for this centurion, but there was more to come. Darkness fell across the land at the sixth hour. That was noon in Jewish time-keeping. That darkness didn't last for only a few minutes; it lasted for three hours and only began to go away brief moments before Jesus died. The centurion had seen darkness, but he had never seen darkness like this. This was the darkest of all darknesses. In the words of William Hendriksen, it was "intense and unforgettable."

And then there was the earthquake that occurred at the very moment that Jesus died (v. 54). All that the centurion had seen and heard converged upon him in a powerful way. Jesus wasn't just another man dying another death. He was the God-man. The centurion wasn't alone in drawing this conclusion; his soldiers drew it as well.

Some say we shouldn't make too much of what this centurion said. They contend that he was only acknowledging that Jesus was a special man.

I don't doubt for a moment that his confession came from a heart that had been touched and transformed by the grace of God. It makes sense to me that Jesus' death would immediately achieve the end for which it was intended, that is, salvation for both Jews and Gentiles. The former is pictured for us by the saved thief and the latter by the centurion.

Yes, I'm sure this centurion came to real faith in Christ, and I'm also sure that his confession is here to make all of us ask ourselves if we have also come to real faith in the Lord Jesus. Have you come to Him as the Son of God, your Savior and Lord, in repentance and faith?

-23-

From God's Word, the Bible...

But the angel answered and said to the women, "Do not be afraid, for I know that you seek Jesus who was crucified. He is not here; for He is risen, as He said. Come, see the place where the Lord lay."

Matthew 28:5-6

"He Is Not Here"
(An Angel)

If a fitly spoken word is an apple of gold in a setting of silver, we have from an angel one of the greatest of all such apples. These words were spoken on the first day of a new week.

The week preceding it had taken the followers of Jesus from "Hallelujah" to horror. The "Hallelujah" part came when Jesus triumphantly rode into Jerusalem. The horror part came when He was arrested, scourged, ridiculed, and crucified.

This new week had to be better even though it was beginning in a sad way with some women making their way to Jesus' tomb with various spices to further anoint His body (Mark 16:1; Luke 24:1).

Their sadness was mingled with anxiety about the huge stone that had been used to seal Jesus' tomb (Mark 16:3). How would they ever manage to roll it away so they could gain access to the body?

Their sadness and anxiety would soon vanish—the anxiety when they saw the stone had been rolled away; the sadness when they realized that there was no dead body to anoint.

They didn't immediately connect the moved stone with Jesus' resurrection. An angel was there at the tomb to make the connection for them, and he did so in these plain and powerful words: "He is not here; for He is risen, as He said" (Matt. 27:6).

The angels of heaven were associated with all of the great redemptive events. An angel announced Jesus' birth to Joseph (Matt. 1:20-25). Gabriel announced Jesus' birth to Mary (Luke 1:26-38). When Jesus was born, a single angel appeared to make the announcement to shepherds outside Bethlehem (Luke 2:11). After the announcement was made, the one angel was joined by "a multitude of the heavenly host praising God" (Luke 2:13). Angels "came and ministered" to Jesus after He was tempted by Satan in the wilderness (Matt. 4:11). In the midst of Jesus' agony in Gethsemane, an angel "appeared to Him from heaven, strengthening Him" (Luke 22:43).

The angels of heaven must have hovered near as the events in Gethsemane and on Golgotha unfolded because Jesus said He could at any moment call twelve legions of them (Matt. 26:53). And the angels would be present when the Lord Jesus ascended to heaven (Acts 1:10-11). So, it is certainly no surprise to find angels present at Jesus' resurrection.

The fact that the angels were present at every point along redemption's road speaks volumes about the nature of redemption. Angels are glorious, magnificent beings. If the work of redemption required their presence all along the way, it must also be glorious and magnificent. Do we see the glory of redemption? The angels are so fascinated by the redemption of sinners that they desire to look into it (1 Peter 2:12). Does God's work of saving sinners fascinate us?

There was a bit of rebuke and a lot of assurance in the angel's words to the women. The rebuke is contained in the words "as He said." The women deserved the rebuke. They should have recalled Jesus' promise that He would rise and they should have come to the tomb, not in somber gloom, but with eager expectation. But to their shame, they weren't expecting the resurrection.

The assurance lay in this flat assertion: "He is not here." And it lay in this invitation: "Come, see the place where the Lord lay." There can be a world of significance in a simple verb tense. The angel didn't ask them to see where the Lord was "lying," but where the Lord "lay." "Lying" would have meant He was still there. "Lay" meant He was no longer there.

The angel's message to the women sent them away from that empty tomb "with fear and great joy" (v. 8). They were filled with awe and overwhelmed with joy. The fact that we are two thousand years removed from the event doesn't make it any less marvelous. Shouldn't we also be filled with awe and joy?

The words of many are reported in the Bible. Some of those words are equal in greatness to the words spoken by this angel on the day of Jesus' resurrection. But none is greater. Sin, death, and hell hadn't won. Jesus was victorious over all, and all who know Him through faith share in that victory.

-24-

From God's Word, the Bible...

And while they looked steadfastly toward heaven as He went up, behold, two men stood by them in white apparel, who also said, "Men of Galilee, why do you stand gazing up into heaven? This same Jesus, who was taken up from you into heaven, will so come in like manner as you saw Him go into heaven."

Acts 1:10-11

"This Same Jesus... Will So Come" (Two Angels)

Days of gladness, days of sadness! Those were the days between Jesus' resurrection and His ascension. The gladness came from the fact that Jesus had gloriously triumphed over the grave. His disciples, slow to believe His promise that He would rise again, were surprised and overjoyed when He did.

But the gladness of those post-resurrection days had to be mingled with sadness as the disciples realized that Jesus would soon leave them once again. The dreaded day arrived—all too quickly in their estimation—and Jesus, after speaking words of assurance to them (vv. 4-5,7-8), was suddenly "taken up" and a cloud received Him out of their sight" (v. 9).

The dreaded moment had come. Jesus was gone, and His disciples must have felt a desperate yearning for Him as they stood staring at that spot where they had last seen Him.

Comfort is what those disciples needed at that moment, and comfort is what they received. The comfort came in the form of two men who weren't really men. Their "white apparel" (v. 10) should make us think of John 20:12, which speaks of "two angels in white" who were sitting in the tomb where Jesus' body had lain.

Angels had come to the sad disciples to give them the assurance that the Jesus who had been taken from them would come again.

There was certainly much in what the angels said to thrill those disciples, and there is much to thrill us if we are Jesus' disciples.

The first thrill is in the "will." The word "will" leaves no room for uncertainty, and that is the word the angels used in regard to Jesus coming again. It will happen.

Many centuries have come and gone since the angels used their "will," and many are the scoffers who cry: "Where is the promise of His coming?" (2 Peter 3:4). These scoffers suggest that the length of time between the promise and its fulfillment negates the promise. To them, the fact that the fulfillment has been so long in coming means it won't come.

The Apostle Peter, who heard the angels deliver their message on that long-ago day, informs us that God doesn't reckon time as we do. What seems to be a very long period of time to us is short to Him (2 Peter 3:8). And Peter assures us that the Lord "is not slack concerning His promise." His delay in fulfilling it doesn't mean it won't be fulfilled. God delays it so He can bring more sinners to repentance (2 Peter 3:9).

Let's not allow ourselves to be influenced by the skeptics but continue to believe with firm faith that the angels' "will" will be fulfilled.

The second thrill in the angels' words to the disciples is in the word "same." The same Jesus who was taken from them that day is the very One who would come for them. It would be the very Jesus whom they had known and loved during His earthly ministry. It would be the Jesus who had been nailed to the cross. It would be the Jesus who was raised from the dead. The Jesus who had come to this earth in our humanity and who had died and risen again in that humanity will come in that same humanity. We will be able to recognize Him by the nail prints in His hands and feet.

The fact that Jesus has gone into heaven in our humanity and will come again in that same humanity means that all of His people will eventually follow Him into heaven in their humanity. Heaven won't be a place where people float around like so many wisps of smoke. It will be God's people dwelling on a new earth in resurrected, glorified bodies.

All of the men and women who saw Jesus ascend to heaven eventually died. Does that mean the angels' promise about Jesus coming again failed for those who died? To the contrary, they will have an advantage when Jesus comes because "the dead in Christ will rise first" (1 Thess. 4:16).

Jesus' coming again will mean resurrection for dead believers and immediate translation from earth to heaven for living believers (1 Thess. 4:17).

What glory awaits those who belong to Christ! We should look forward to it with eager expectation, knowing that we have in the promise of those two angels a true apple of gold in a setting of silver.

-25-

From God's Word, the Bible...

So they said, "Believe on the Lord Jesus Christ, and you will be saved, you and your household."

Acts 16:31

Paul Speaks to a Jailer

Paul and Silas were in prison. The reason? Paul had in the name of Jesus cast a demon out of a young girl (vv. 16-18). Her masters were enraged. They had been using her fortune telling as a way to make a lot of money (vv. 16,19). So these masters complained to the magistrates about Paul and Silas: "These men, being Jews, exceedingly trouble our city" (v. 20).

We should also note that the masters of the young girl had been able to whip a "multitude" into frenzied opposition toward Paul and Silas (v. 22). The magistrates caved in. Setting aside legal proceedings, they ordered Paul and Silas to be beaten and imprisoned (v. 23).

In pain from "many stripes," in prison, and in stocks in the prison! (vv. 23-24)—what a horrible situation for Paul and Silas!

There are several amazing things in this account. It's amazing that Paul could cast out a demon in the name of

Jesus. It's amazing that Paul's act could incite so much hatred. It's amazing that the authorities scorned due process and subjected Paul and Silas to such inhumane treatment. But the most amazing thing in my book is this: "But at midnight Paul and Silas were praying and singing hymns to God, and the prisoners were listening to them" (v. 25).

Gordon Keddie says of them: "They had been beaten up, but they were not beaten down!"[3]

The singing and praying of Paul and Silas abruptly ended when "a great earthquake" occurred, throwing all the doors open and snapping all the prisoners' chains (v. 26).

With his prison in shambles and his prisoners gone, the jailer went from earthquake to heart quake. He had been sternly commanded to keep Paul and Silas "securely" (v. 23). He knew his life would count for theirs, so in a flash of despair, he decided to end his life then and there. But wait! The prisoners weren't gone! How he must have rejoiced to hear Paul's loud cry: "Do yourself no harm, for we are all here" (v. 28).

This jailer had almost stepped over the thin line that separates this world from the eternal world. He was suddenly hit with the realization that he had almost stepped into an eternity for which he wasn't prepared. So he "called for a light, ran in, and fell down trembling before Paul and Silas" (v. 29). He then brought them out of the rubble and asked: "Sirs, what must I do to be saved?" (v. 30).

We shouldn't be surprised that he asked this question. God had used the praying and singing of Paul and Silas and the shaking of the earth to make this man realize that they had something he didn't have—and something he urgently needed.

Paul didn't fumble or mumble when the jailer asked his

---

[3] Gordon J. Keddie, *You are My Witnesses* (Welwyn Commentary Series), Evangelical Press, 2000, p. 191.

question. He quickly gave the jailer this very plain and simple word: "Believe on the Lord Jesus Christ, and you will be saved, you and your household" (v. 31).

Paul and Silas soon amplified that abbreviated statement as "they spoke the word of the Lord to him and to all who were in his house" (v. 32).

There are three indications that the jailer immediately complied with Paul's words and believed in the Lord Jesus Christ. He took Paul and Silas into his home where he treated their wounds and provided food for them. He and his household were baptized. And he rejoiced in the salvation that he had received (v. 34).

This account speaks with power to believers in Christ. It tells us that we must make it our business to be happy Christians so the Lord can use us as He did Paul and Silas. Every difficulty that comes our way gives us the opportunity to show unbelievers the difference our Christianity makes. This story also shows us that we should always be ready to tell those around us what is necessary for them to be saved.

This story also speaks with power to unbelievers, affirming that the only way to be saved is to believe in the Lord Jesus. No matter how great a sinner one has been, there is salvation for him or her in Christ.

I wouldn't have enjoyed being with Paul and Silas in that prison. But I certainly would have enjoyed hearing Paul say: "Believe on the Lord Jesus Christ, and you will be saved. . . ."

-26-

From God's Word, the Bible...

"I, Jesus, have sent My angel to testify to you these things in the churches. I am the Root and the Offspring of David, the Bright and Morning Star."

Revelation 22:16

The Next-to-Last Words of Jesus

The last recorded words of Jesus in the Bible are found in verse 20 of Revelation 22. We shall come to those. In this reading, we are giving our attention to the next-to-last words of Jesus. They are recorded for us in Revelation 22:16. We might describe this verse as a ton of truth in a small package.

The Lord Jesus is speaking about Himself in this verse. What He has to say should delight each and every child of God. We should note that He begins by calling Himself "Jesus." Here He is appearing to John in all of His glory, and He isn't ashamed of the name that He bore during His time on this earth. That name was associated with all the suffering that He had to endure. It is especially connected with His suffering on the cross. When He was crucified, the placard above His head had these words: "Jesus of Nazareth, the King of the Jews" (John 19:19).

The conclusion we draw is most precious indeed, and

that is that Jesus, now in glory, isn't ashamed to be known as Jesus. He is unashamed of His human name because He has carried our humanity into heaven. How often we miss this! Jesus has carried our humanity into heaven! He isn't there now in exactly the same way that He was before He came to this earth. When He took our humanity, He took it forever. And His presence in heaven in our humanity is the guarantee that all who believe in Him will finally follow Him into heaven in resurrected, glorified humanity.

The next thing we should notice is the phrase "My angel." The truth is that the Lord has many angels. The fact that these splendid beings readily and eagerly do His will conveys to us how great our Lord is. He is even now our reigning Lord. The fact that He often doesn't appear to be reigning doesn't mean that He isn't. We will understand it better by and by.

There's yet another phrase that calls for our attention: "to testify to you these things in the churches." While John penned the book of Revelation, he wasn't really the author of it. It was the revelation of the Lord Jesus through John to the churches. It was the Lord testifying to the seven churches that originally received it and to all churches since.

The thing for us to carry away from this is the concern and care that the Lord Jesus has for His churches. When He left this world, He ascended to join His Father in the glories of heaven. But that doesn't mean He washed His hands of what is going on with His people in this world. Nothing that goes on in His churches is unimportant to Him.

This verse comes to a close with Jesus asserting that He is "the Root and Offspring of David, the Bright and Morning Star."

The first of these two titles, "the Root and Offspring of David," affirms that Jesus is both God and man. The "Root" part of that title means that the Lord Jesus was both the

Creator and the Savior of David. In other words, the Lord was the source of both the physical and the spiritual life of David. The "Offspring" part of that title means Jesus, in fulfillment of prophecy, descended from David. To be David's "Root," Jesus had to be God. To be his "Offspring," Jesus had to be a man.

"The Bright and Morning Star" is a marvelous title. Does that mean that Jesus gives light? Yes. But all stars do that. This is a special kind of star. It announces and introduces the coming of day. The Lord Jesus Christ will bring all of His people into never-ending day in heaven. Don Fortner splendidly writes:

> In that great day, our great Saviour will bring all things to light, and we shall see all things clearly. Then, but not until then, shall we understand all the purposes of God, all the dispensations of providence, all the work of redemption, all the fullness of the covenant, all the glory of grace—and why he saved us.[4]

It has often been said that last words are very special, and they are. But in the case of the Lord Jesus, I must say that next-to-last words are very special also.

---

[4] Don Fortner, *Discovering Christ in Revelation*, Evangelical Press, 2002, p. 486.

-27-

From God's Word, the Bible...

And the Spirit and the bride say, "Come!" And let him who hears say, "Come!" And let him who thirsts come. Whoever desires, let him take the water of life freely.

Revelation 22:17

A Word from the Holy Spirit

Given the fact that the whole Bible was inspired by the Holy Spirit, we could say the Holy Spirit has spoken a lot. But the Holy Spirit rarely quotes Himself in Scripture. We do have in the verse before us one quote from the Holy Spirit. A simple quote it is, consisting of only one word—"Come!" Since the Lord Jesus spoke in the preceding verse, it only makes sense for the Holy Spirit to urge us to come to Jesus.

It is the unique and special work of the Spirit to exalt the Lord Jesus and to call sinners to Him.

The Spirit's call is warmhearted. "Come" is a warm word. It isn't threatening or frightening.

The Spirit's call is also wide. All are invited to come to Christ. He is the "water of life" (John 4:13-14; 7:37-38) of which we may freely drink, so come and drink freely! The only condition is to be thirsty. Thirsty for forgiveness! Thirsty for right standing with God! Thirsty for eternal life in heaven! If you are thirsty, come and drink! If you are still breathing and still thinking, it isn't too late to come to Christ.

Satan convinces many to refuse the Spirit's invitation because they have been such horrible sinners. Satan tells them that Jesus is only a Savior for those who don't need much saving. He asserts that Jesus is the Savior for only some sinners. In addition to being a colossal lie, that is a despicable insult to Jesus. It suggests that He is a limited and inadequate Savior. Meanwhile, the Bible insists that Jesus can and does save all those who come to Him, no matter how they have plumbed the depths of wickedness. The author of Hebrews writes: ". . . He is also able to save to the uttermost those who come to God through Him, since He ever lives to make intercession for them" (Heb. 7:25).

The word "uttermost" isn't commonly used, but in reference to this matter of salvation, it is one wonderful word. It tells us that the Lord Jesus receives those who are deepest in sin and who are farthest away, and saves them completely and forever.

Jesus Himself expressed the wideness of His salvation when He said: "Come to Me, all you who labor and are heavy laden, and I will give you rest" (Matt. 11:28).

The condition here is that we "labor and are heavy laden." If we're burdened with the weight and the guilt of our sins, we can come to the Lord Jesus with the confidence that He will give us rest. It is not required that we be good sinners or little sinners to be saved—only that we be sinners. These words from Julia H. Johnston express this truth very well.

Marvelous grace of our loving Lord,
Grace that exceeds our sin and our guilt!
Yonder on Calvary's mount outpoured,
There where the blood of the Lamb was spilled.

> *Grace, grace, God's grace,*
> *Grace that will pardon and cleanse within;*
> *Grace, grace, God's grace,*
> *Grace that is greater than all our sin!*
> *Marvelous, infinite, matchless grace,*
> *Freely bestowed on all who believe!*
> *You that are longing to see His face,*
> *Will you this moment His grace receive?*

The only limit imposed on the Lord's ability to save is the one that we ourselves impose by refusing to come to Him.

In addition to the wideness of the invitation, this verse mentions a wideness in the proclamation of the Lord's saving grace. The Spirit urges sinners to come to Christ, and He is joined in that urging by the bride of Christ, that is, by the church. The work of the church is to proclaim the gospel far and wide and to urge sinners to accept it. Many churches and pastors need to be reminded of this.

There's yet more. The individual who has heeded the invitation of the Spirit and the church to come to Christ is invited again—this time to join the Spirit and the church and say to those who are still outside of Christ: "Come!"

To come to Christ means we repent of our sins and trust completely in what He has done for sinners. With the single word "Come," the Holy Spirit calls us to repentance and faith. He calls us to Christ and salvation. He calls us to heaven. What a lovely, delightful word the Holy Spirit has given us! It is an apple of gold.

-28-

From God's Word, the Bible...

He who testifies to these things says,
"Surely I am coming quickly."
Amen. Even so, come, Lord Jesus!

Revelation 22:20

The Last Words of Jesus

This is a special verse. It relates the last words spoken by Jesus in the Bible: "Surely, I am coming quickly." This is the third and final time that Jesus spoke these words. The first time is in verse 7, and the second is in verse 12. The threefold repetition was Jesus' way of emphasizing truth that His people urgently needed.

We must always keep in mind that the book of Revelation was addressed to seven churches in Asia Minor (1:11). These churches were facing trying circumstances and serious challenges. The whole book was designed to give them comfort and encouragement, but they must have found Jesus' assurance that He was coming quickly to be particularly so.

It may seem at first glance that Jesus' words weren't true. Two thousand years have come and gone since Jesus spoke those words. That certainly doesn't seem to equal a quick coming.

One way to deal with this dilemma is to say that Jesus isn't dealing with how soon He will come, but rather the way that He will come when He comes. In other words, when the time finally arrives for Him to come, it will happen very quickly. He will appear without delay and will come in such a way that people will be taken by surprise. And the change that His people will experience will occur "in the twinkling of an eye" (1 Cor. 15:52).

But look again at Jesus' words, and note the present tense. He doesn't say: "I will come." That would certainly be a true statement, but that's not what He says. He says: "Surely, I am coming quickly."

The second coming of Jesus isn't just an event that has to occur. It is a process that has to unfold. That process is laid out for us in Revelation in the form of seven seals, seven trumpets, and seven bowls. Each of these seals, trumpets, and bowls represents God working in history to move us ever closer to the coming of His Son.

The actual event in which Jesus comes has not occurred quickly, but the process that leads to His coming has been unfolding in rapid fashion since the hour that Jesus ascended to the Father in heaven. History hasn't been standing still; it has been steadily marching toward its end.

It's very easy for us to concern ourselves with the wrong thing in regard to the Lord's coming. We tend to get engrossed with the timing of it. We read the word "quickly," and we immediately get caught up in the debate as to whether that is true or false. Jesus quite clearly put the emphasis on a totally different matter—our obedience to His commandments. In verse 7, He says: "Blessed is he who keeps the words of the prophecy of this book." In verse 12, He says: "My reward is with Me, to give to every one according to his work."

When the Bible deals with the Lord's return, it doesn't

lay the stress on *when* but rather on *how*. It doesn't encourage us to ask when the Lord's coming will occur. It rather encourages us to ask ourselves how we are living. Are we tampering and trifling with His Word or giving serious and careful attention to it? Are we mindful of the fact that obedience will bring rich rewards from our Lord, and disobedience will cause the loss of those rewards?

To put it another way, the truth of the Lord's coming ought to make us think seriously and carefully about these words from the Apostle Peter: ". . .what manner of persons ought you to be in holy conduct and godliness. . ." (2 Peter 3:11).

The last recorded words of Jesus—how encouraging they are! The Lord Jesus is even now in the process of coming. World events are not meaningless. The Lord is working in and through them to prepare the stage for His appearance. Our response to these things should be to say: "Are You, Lord, in the process of coming? Continue the process until it is finally complete, and we finally see Your dear face in glory." In other words, our response should be to join John in saying: "Amen. Even so, come Lord Jesus!"

-29-

From God's Word, the Bible...

And one of them, Caiaphas, being high priest that year, said to them, "You know nothing at all, nor do you consider that it is expedient for us that one man should die for the people, and not that the whole nation should perish."

John 11:49-50

An Apple of Gold from a Rotten Apple (1)

Sometimes truth comes from unusual places. In the verses above, the Gospel of John gives us a couple of examples of this. Caiaphas and Pilate were anything but good men. They weren't men who had a close and familiar association with the truth. But on the occasions reported in these verses, they spoke marvelous truths about Jesus. It is always an apple of gold when the truth is spoken about Jesus. So, Caiaphas and Pilate give us apples of gold even though they were rotten apples.

We will look at Pilate in our next reading. Let me introduce you now to Caiaphas. Don't shake his hand. If you do, you will have to immediately wash your hand. This Caiaphas was one slimy fellow. It wouldn't seem so. It shouldn't have been so. Caiaphas was holding the highest office that Jewish religion had to offer. He was the high priest. A man holding such a high office should be high in virtue and integrity. Not Caiaphas! This man treasured murder in his heart, and urged others to treasure it as well.

Jesus had just raised Lazarus from the dead even though he had been in the grave for four days. That act put the cat among the pigeons. It caused many to believe in Jesus (v. 45). The religious leaders of Israel knew they had to do something about Jesus. If they left Him alone, more and more would follow Him, and when the Romans learned that multitudes of Jews were acknowledging Jesus as their king, well, they wouldn't be happy.

The dilemma of what to do with Jesus prompted Caiaphas to offer his murderous assessment: Jesus must die! Caiaphas was speaking as a political man who was concerned with political realities, but he inadvertently spoke the truth. Here's part of what he said: ". . . it is expedient that one man should die for the people, and not that the whole nation should perish" (v. 50).

To Caiaphas, it was Jesus or the nation. If Jesus didn't die, the nation would, and he, Caiaphas, would much sooner part with Jesus than with the nation.

John, the author of this Gospel, couldn't wait to jump on that. After relating Caiaphas' words, John quickly added these words: "Now this he did not say on his own authority; but being high priest that year he prophesied that Jesus would die for the nation, and not for that nation only, but also that He would gather together in one the children of God who were scattered abroad" (vv. 51-52).

In trying to rid himself of Jesus, Caiaphas had preached the gospel! Had he realized it, he would have been mortified. Had he realized his blunder, he might have felt like removing his unruly tongue so he could never repeat the blunder again.

There have been many wonderful preachers of the

gospel through the centuries. The names of George Whitefield, Charles Spurgeon, Jonathan Edwards, and Martyn Lloyd-Jones easily come to mind. Should we add Caiaphas to that list? Imagine it! Caiaphas, a preacher of the gospel! Who could have guessed it?

But, of course, Caiaphas didn't preach the gospel knowingly and willingly. He blundered into the truth of the gospel. He didn't speak "on his own authority." It was God who was speaking through the evil Caiaphas at this moment.

What is the gospel? It is the good news of Jesus dying for others so they don't have to die. It is Jesus dying as a substitute for others. It is as Caiaphas said!

We aren't talking here about Jesus dying physically so others wouldn't have to die physically. It is much more profound than that. We're talking about Jesus dying a special kind of death—one in which He received the wrath of God that sinners themselves will receive in eternity if they don't receive Him.

We don't know what became of Caiaphas. We can hope that, after Jesus died, he recalled his own words and understood them, not in the political way that he originally had in mind, but rather on the higher level of Jesus dying as the substitute for sinners. We can hope that Caiaphas came to believe that Jesus died for him and that he laid hold of that with real faith. We can hope that Caiaphas will be in heaven. While we wait to see if he is, let's rejoice in the apple of gold that he left us in a setting of silver—his statement of the gospel.

-30-

From God's Word, the Bible...

Pilate said to Him, "What is truth?" And when he had said this,
he went out again to the Jews, and said to them,
"I find no fault in Him at all."

John 18:38

An Apple of Gold from a Rotten Apple (2)

Pontius Pilate was the big Roman in the land of Israel. He governed the Jews as the representative of the Roman Empire. When we meet him in John's Gospel, he has a very complex problem on his hands—Jesus!

The religious leaders of the Jews had taken Jesus into custody, had "tried" Him and found Him worthy of death. But the Jews weren't to execute criminals without approval from Rome. So, they brought Jesus to Pilate along with a charge that they knew would resonate with Pilate, namely, that Jesus was claiming to be a king (Luke 23:2). A Roman governor would have to take that seriously because Caesar didn't like having rival kings around. So Pilate began his interrogation of Jesus by asking Him: "Are you the King of the Jews?" (v. 33).

After interrogating Jesus three times, Pilate said to the

Jewish leaders: "I find no fault in Him." Pilate certainly didn't intend those words to be a theological statement about Jesus. He was merely concerned with legalities and politics. He was merely offering his assessment that there was no legal basis for even holding Jesus, much less for executing Him.

As far as theological truth was concerned, Pilate couldn't have cared less. A few minutes before announcing his finding to the Jews, Pilate had walked away from Jesus with a casual shrug and the question: "What is truth?" (v. 38).

But while Pilate didn't intend to make a theological statement about Jesus, that's exactly what he did. There is no fault to be found in Jesus. There was no legal fault to be found in Jesus. He hadn't broken any of Rome's laws. But we must go further. There is no moral fault in Jesus. He was completely without sin. Jesus is the only person who has lived perfectly. He never thought an evil thought, never spoke a wrong word, and never did a sinful thing. He is, in the words of the Apostle Peter, "a lamb without blemish and without spot" (1 Peter 1:19).

There was a time in which most professing Christians considered the sinless life of Jesus to be an indispensable link in the chain of redemption. Several years ago, most Christians would have readily agreed that if the link of Jesus' sinlessness is broken, the whole of redemption is irretrievably broken. But things have changed. Surveys in recent years have revealed serious slippage at this point with many who profess faith in Christ now saying He probably committed sins, or, to put it in a more sanitary fashion, "made mistakes."

Count me among those who are unwilling to give up the sinlessness of Christ, and among those who believe that it is still an essential link in the chain of redemption. To me, it is quite simple. Jesus came to this earth to pay the penalty for sinners. If He had been guilty of sin Himself, He would have had to pay the penalty for Himself and, therefore, could not have paid the penalty for others.

We must always keep this in mind: part of what Jesus came to this earth to do was to provide the very righteousness that God demands of sinners. God requires it, but we don't' have it. Jesus, on the other hand, did have it, and God in grace counts the righteousness of Christ as though it were ours when we come to Christ in repentance and faith.

Jesus gave testimony to His own sinlessness when He boldly asked the religious leaders this question: "Which of you convicts Me of sin?" (John 8:46a). Jesus could never have asked that question if He had the slightest bit of uncertainty about His performance. The fact that He did ask it tells us that He knew there was no sin to be found in Him. A bit earlier, He had said to those same men: "I always do those things that please Him" (v. 29). And the "Him" to whom He was referring was His Father.

This wasn't brazen arrogance on the part of Jesus. It was merely a statement of fact. We should accept it as a fact and rejoice in it.

Are we grateful that Pilate had no interest in discovering the truth about Jesus? No, but we should be grateful that, in the midst of His political maneuverings, He stated for us the truth about Jesus. There was no fault in Jesus, but there is fault in us; that's why we need a sinless, perfect Savior such as Jesus. Is He your Lord and Savior? Have you turned from sin and are you trusting in Him alone?

-31-

From God's Word, the Bible...

Now the serpent was more cunning than any beast of the field which the LORD God had made. And he said to the woman, "Has God indeed said, 'You shall not eat of every tree of the garden'?"

Then the serpent said to the woman, "You will not surely die. For God knows that in the day you eat of it your eyes will be opened, and you will be like God, knowing good and evil."

Genesis 3:1, 4-5

A Truly Rotten Apple from A Truly Rotten Apple

It has been our blessing and privilege to notice several fitly spoken words in the Bible. The Book of Proverbs calls these "apples of gold." Jesus spoke most of the words we have noticed. That shouldn't surprise us. Jesus, the greatest person who ever lived, spoke the greatest words ever spoken. But we have also found opportunities to notice words from the Father, the Holy Spirit, angels, and men. We have even come across a couple of apples of gold from very evil men.

We now come to the end of this volume by listening to someone we have not yet heard from—Satan. In the opening verses of Genesis 3, we come upon Satan speaking. His words are as distorted as he is. They can never be called "apples of gold." It is far more fitting to refer to his words as rotten words. Since he is such a thoroughly rotten being, we have in his words a truly rotten apple from a truly rotten apple. His words were rotten because they came from his rotten mouth.

Satan is still speaking rotten words. He does so when he prompts people to indulge in blasphemy, profanity, gossip, and complaining. He is very active in prompting ministers to distort and deny the gospel of Christ. But Satan has never spoken more rotten, evil words than he did in the garden of Eden. Those words were spoken to an audience of one, but they have affected every human being since.

Satan came to Eve in the form of a serpent, which may have originally been the most beautiful of all the animals God made. By coming in this attractive form, Satan was probably hoping to catch Eve off guard.

The first rotten words Satan spoke questioned the goodness of God: "Has God indeed said, 'You shall not eat of every tree of the garden'?" (v. 1). Satan was insinuating that God wasn't as good as Adam and Eve thought Him to be. He was holding something back from them! A truly good God would deny them nothing! He would have given them access to every single tree of the garden without so much as a single exception.

Satan still enjoys attacking the goodness of God. When a difficulty comes our way, he is quick to say: "Ah, you see, you are facing this thing because God doesn't really care for you."

Sadly enough, multitudes of people believe his lie.

The next rotten words that came from Satan's mouth flatly denied the truth of God's Word. When Satan asked if Eve was free to eat of all the trees of the garden, she replied: "We may eat the fruit of the trees of the garden; but of the fruit of the tree which is in the midst of the garden, God has said, 'You shall not eat it, nor shall you touch it, lest you die'" (vv. 2-3).

That was fairly close to being accurate. God had

definitely told Adam and Eve to not eat of the tree, but, so far as we know, He hadn't told them to not touch it (2:17).

Satan's response was swift and brazen: "You will not surely die" (v. 4).

God had spoken, and Satan contradicted Him. Satan is still doing this. Every denial of the truth of God's Word has his leering face behind it.

Yes, God had forbidden Adam and Eve to eat of the tree of knowledge of good and evil, but it wasn't to be unkind to them. He made them with free will. For the will to be truly free, it has to have a choice to make. God could have made Adam and Eve mere machines that had no choice but to love and obey Him. But He made them so they would have to choose to obey Him. The fact that God made them this way was an expression of His goodness to them—just the opposite of what Satan said.

And, yes, the penalty for their disobedience was death in all of its forms—physical, spiritual, and eternal. Spiritual death was the central thing. It is alienation from God and it results in physical and eternal death.

Satan's words to Eve were the rottenest ever spoken because they brought death upon Adam and Eve and all their descendants. But good came from those rotten words. In response to them, God answered with this apple of gold— "Christ!"

As we draw this book to a conclusion, let us think of One who was to come as the Second Adam and who would be the Savior of sinners—the Lord Jesus Christ. Satan tried to tempt Him, too, but without any success. God was true to His promise that Jesus would crush the head of Satan. He did that at Calvary when He bore the sins of all who would ever turn away from sin and trust Him as Lord and Savior. And He still saves sinners today. Has He saved you? He is a willing and able Savior. Come to Him in repentance and faith right now!

About the Author

Roger Ellsworth is a retired pastor, active in ministry and writing, who lives in Jackson, Tennessee. He and his wife, Sylvia, love the message of the Bible, and they enjoy sharing the wonderful counsel of the Word of God in language that ordinary people can understand and appreciate.

Roger has written numerous books on the Christian faith, and has exercised a preaching ministry for over fifty years. His sermons are available to listen for free on SermonAudio.com.

The Series

Enjoy collecting the My Coffee Cup Meditations Series.

A Dog and A Clock 978-0-9988812-9-4 (Series#1)
The "Thumbs-Up" Man 978-0-9988812-5-6 (Series#2)
When God Blocks Our Path 978-0-9988812-4-9 (Series#3)
Fading Lines, Unfading Hope 978-0-9996559-1-7 (Series#4)
The Day the Milk Spilled 978-0-9965168-6-0 (Series#5)
"Where Are the Donuts?" 978-0-9965168-7-7 (Series#6)
Sure Signs of Heavenly Hope 978-0-9988812-1-8 (Series#7)
My Dog Knows It's Sunday 978-0-9996559-6-2 (Series#8)
Rover and the Cows 978-0-9996559-7-9 (Series#9)
Apples of Gold in Silver Settings 978-0-9600203-0-0 (Series#10)
Old Houses, New Houses 978-0-9600203-1-7 (Series#11)
Golden Key and Silver Chain 978-0-9600203-2-4 (Series#12)

Get the set for a special price:

www.mycoffeecupmeditations.com/crazyoffer

Collect All the Books!

www.mycoffeecupmeditations.com

www.ingramcontent.com/pod-product-compliance
Lightning Source LLC
Chambersburg PA
CBHW050555300426
44112CB00013B/1930